Emotional Survival

To order additional copies, please contact us.
BookSurge, LLC
www.booksurge.com
1-866-308-6235
orders@booksurge.com

CHRISTINA STRAKES, PH.D.

EMOTIONAL SURVIVAL

2007

Emotional Survival

CONTENTS

Page

ACKNOWLEDGEMENTS

There are several people who made this book possible. The first is my very loving, intelligent, and remarkable mother, Jean Spotts Strakes. Without her steadfast dedication and support this book would not have come into fruition. I owe her so much for her input, editing, and general willingness to travel with me on this literary journey.

I must also acknowledge my family, i.e. aunts and cousins, for without their cruel insensitivity this book might not have been written.

Finally, I must thank the mentors, professors, and friends who inspired and helped me to become a Psychologist. I thank Dr. Marvin Sontag, Dr. Winthrop Adkins, Dr. Roger Myers, Dr. Paul Vahanian, Dr. Joyce Meyerhardt and Dr. Yelena Kazakina. I want to also thank Dr. Gregory Reising, and Dr. Doris Morgan.

CHRISTINA STRAKES, Ph.D.

*I Dedicate This Book To My Mother, Jean Spotts Strakes,
And To The Memories Of My Grandmother, Anna
Stratakis, And Of My Aunt, Lella Stratakis.
I Also Dedicate This Book To Every Person Who Has
Suffered More Than His Or Her Fair Share Of Emotional
Pain And Sorrow.*

INTRODUCTION

Many individuals feel a void in their lives, a vague discontent they cannot describe, while many others are struggling with profound feelings of loneliness and depression without really knowing why. Some of these individuals are baby boomers who have reached the age where they are becoming more reflective of the time they have lived and the time they have left.

No matter how reflective we may be, or how hard we may try to understand this life, many questions confound the human mind because they are too incomprehensible to grasp, e.g. creation, gestation, astronomy, and death.

In addition to living with existential uncertainty, we must also live with the pervasive uncertainty of today's troubled world, that is, the ominous threats of terrorism, biological attacks, nuclear war, etc. Add to this the trials and tribulations in our personal life and it is easy to see why some of us seek an escape from reality or some form of protective armor, and this need for emotional protection is more compelling today than ever before.

We do not exist in a vacuum so we are deeply affected by the environmental conditions that surround us and the cultural values which are taught to us by our society. Moreover, we are repeatedly exposed to a floodgate of incomprehensible human cruelties that overwhelm our basic need to make sense of reality. How are we supposed to understand a mother strapping her two young children into the back of a car and then pushing the car into the water as she hears them crying for "Mommy"? How do we comprehend a man lining up 12 small children against the wall and shooting them in the back of their heads? How can we make sense of the terrorists who crashed those airplanes into the Twin Towers on September 11, 2001, and all the other terrorists who blow themselves up to kill as many innocent people as they can? We may think we are detached from these human cruelties but we are not for they make an indelible mark on our sense of emotional security and psychological well being.

This book addresses the profound impact that our complex society and troubled world have on our emotional well-being. Several renowned authors have written extensively on this point but their collective wisdom has never been collated or brought together before in any single literary work until now. In a very highly selective manner and in easy to understand language, this book incorporates the wisest and most insightful thinking of the most honored psychologists and psychiatrists of our time, many of whom are looked upon by their colleagues as geniuses.

Finally, this book was written primarily for those who are emotionally wounded and who are struggling to emotionally survive in this increasingly harsh and isolating world. It is a book for those who find themselves emotionally cut off and closed down because of the painful experiences they have endured. In short, it is a book written for those who have been hurt by love and life.

CHAPTER ONE
THE IDEAL SELF

"Today we come across a person who acts and feels like an automaton; who never experiences anything that is really his; who experiences himself entirely as the person he thinks he is supposed to be; whose artificial smile has replaced genuine laughter; whose meaningless chatter has replaced communicative speech; whose dulled despair has taken the place of genuine pain. Two statements can be made about this person. One is that he suffers from a defect of spontaneity and individuality that may seem incurable. At the same time, it may also be said that he does not differ essentially from millions of others."
(Erich Fromm)

Each culture or society superimposes a man-made artificial world onto the natural world in which man lives and we learn very early in life from our man-made world about that which is required for social acceptance and success.[1] We watch, observe, admire, and then attempt to emulate those role models who appear to be the most successful and socially accepted, and these observations have a powerful impact on us as they become ingrained in our unconscious minds.

In essence, we learn about the attributes that will place us high on the social hierarchy and those that do not, and we tend to measure our self-worth according to how well we meet these external socialized criteria. As a result, we attempt to shape and mold our lives, as well as ourselves, in the pursuit of those attributes and qualities that are most esteemed in our society. In short, we learn from our society about that which we need to become. However, when this lesson is based solely on society's coercion rather than our own innate desires, we sacrifice not only our individuality but also our emotional ability to find and/or sustain true inner peace.

Our values, goals, dreams, and expectations, as well as our self-awareness, self-image and self-appraisal, are inseparable from that which we see, hear, and experience in our society.[2] To be separable, that is, to be unaffected by our society's teachings, we must not only have a strong sense of self but we must also continuously exert great effort against its influence. This is not an easy task because it conflicts with our natural innate tendency to adapt to our environment no matter what that environment demands from us. Since we must remain socially connected to our environment, we make great effort - - sometimes lifelong effort - - to adapt, to fit in, and to belong.

Social influences and pressures begin to affect us very early in childhood not only through our social interactions with others but also through exposure to the media, e.g. television, movies, magazines, advertisements, etc. As the socialization process begins, we start formulating beliefs that incorporate specific societal norms and expectations into our minds and personalities.

Erich Fromm, a prominent psychologist, theorized that each society actually establishes in each of its members a shared "social unconscious" which is a socially conditioned filtering process in our minds that allows some thoughts and beliefs to be consciously entertained while other thoughts and beliefs are forced out of awareness.[3] This theory validates how powerful the socialization process is, so much so that it becomes an integral part of our unconscious minds.[4] It is an interesting side note to question the source from which this powerful socialization process emerges. In other words, *who or what is socializing us?*

> *But since every person is blindly convinced that he is nothing but his very modest and unimportant consciousness, which neatly fulfills duties and earns a moderate living, nobody is aware that this whole rationally organized crowd, called a state or a nation (or a society) is run by a seemingly impersonal, imperceptible but terrific power, checked by nobody or nothing. (Carl Jung, 1938, p.60)*

Ironically, this powerful and unidentifiable social force which is checked by nobody or nothing teaches us what is ideal and what we should become. At the same time, it persuades us to conceal what is real within us.

Each of us has a concept of what we would like to be or what we hope we could be, but our concept of what is ideal is determined, in varying degrees, by the society in which we live. Since our society advocates status, attractiveness, and physical fitness, our assessment of how well we fit in and belong, as well as how much power we will have in our lives, is often based on how well we meet these societal expectations.

Our society's concept of what is ideal is consistent and clear. For a man, what is ideal often centers on his income, occupation, and status since he learns very early in life that his worth, power, and desirability are directly tied to his economic status. For a woman, what is ideal often centers on her attractiveness, figure, and sexuality. Since women have been historically portrayed by the media as sexual objects, trophies to be won by men, beauty contestants to appraise and rate, and models to admire and emulate (although men are now being judged in a similar manner) women have been socialized to view their appearance as an indication of their worth - - as *essential* to their worth.

In essence, a woman learns very early in life that her appearance is directly connected to her worth, power, and desirability. Therefore, a woman's excessive preoccupation with her appearance may mask underlying insecurities with regard to her self-worth and lovability.[5] In her mind, the question "Am I attractive?" is inseparable from the question "Am I lovable?"[6] Contrary to what women are socialized to believe, the two questions may be relevant but they are not related. The first question is asking: Am I pretty enough to attract love?[7] The other question is asking: Do I have qualities that make me lovable?[8] Although the first question is important, particularly in younger years, the second question reaches the core of our being and is the one far more relevant to attaining happiness in our lives.[9]

The following genuine responses are by women who illustrate how self-worth and attractiveness can become intertwined. Their names are fictitious.

***

"I learned very early in life that being pretty was important to being loved by a man. This lesson became more ingrained in high school for I could easily see that it was the prettiest girls who got all the boys. I learned from countless magazines that having a small nose and a small waist was essential to being attractive. All my experiences have taught me that beauty is skin deep for most people and rarely, if ever, does anyone look beyond the surface to see what lies beneath." Mary J.

———

"Early in childhood, I began pushing myself hard to achieve and to be perfect. I always felt disappointed in myself in comparison to others... my girlfriends were much prettier than me or they were built much better than me. I had a strong tendency to compare myself to others and always feel disapproval of myself. My clothes were handmade - - not bought at expensive places. As a teenager, I started stealing clothes so I could have nice clothes like the other girls in my class. I had strong feelings of inadequacy in comparison with other girls. As an adult, I still have those same inadequacies. At times, I am envious of other women who are prettier, smarter, wittier, or in any other way, better than I am". Terri K.

***

In this society, our external reality, that is, our income, occupation, status, power, attractiveness, and physique are all of paramount importance with regard to how well we think we are doing in life and how well we feel we fit in and belong. Because we come to value the more superficial aspects of our reality, we also come to value the more superficial aspects of ourselves - - as well as our fellow man. As a result, we are surrounded by that which is superficial, both in feeling and appearance, and this external shallowness further exacerbates our need to conceal what is real within us.

Moreover, because we are socialized to hide our genuine emotions we often interact with others in ways that are inauthentic. Erich Fromm noted, there is not much depth or emotional expression to be found in today's human interactions, but, there is instead, a rather superficial friendliness and a more than superficial courtesy which effectively conceals our underlying mistrust, distance and indifference to each other.[10]

In addition, we are continuously exposed to a media that often portrays a superficial or fabricated reality that is incongruent with our real life circumstances and our true nature. The major limitation with this fabricated reality is that it is not only unrealistic but often not possible. Therefore, our exposure to the more accurate psychological complexities of life and to human imperfection in general is further concealed from our conscious awareness.

Television and movies rarely depict real-life characters who wrestle simultaneously with a multitude of complex emotional issues such as fear, anxiety, injustice, illness, loneliness, and despair. Instead, they often depict heroic characters who are confronted with only one monumental problem and whose lives are otherwise unchallenged and un-conflicted. In the end, the hero always prevails no matter what the odds, and then rides off into the sunset with his one true love to live happily ever after, but we all know that real life is not like this.

In real life we are often bombarded with many problems at once with no possible way to resolve them. We do not win our battles and then ride off into the sunset. Many of us live instead in a quandary filled with obstacles, heartaches and/or difficult circumstances that we cannot resolve or change. So many times, we feel helpless, afraid, and overwhelmed by the demands of living but we experience these feelings only in the privacy of our own lives - - and in our own minds - - which makes us feel even more isolated and alone. We are reluctant to disclose our feelings of fear, anxiety, and depression with others because we think that no one could relate to or understand these emotions. That is why, on those rare occasions when true-to-life characters appear on the screen, viewers become captivated because these characters openly express the emotions that many of us frequently feel but cover up.

The field of advertising is another external influence teaching us that we are not acceptable as we are. Since advertising reflects what a society values, we are bombarded with images of individuals who are extremely attractive, successful, and happy - - all of which perpetuate the illusion of external perfection. In fact, the entire field of advertising is essentially based on appealing to our basic insecurities.

The subliminal message that underlies most advertisements is that we need this product to make us acceptable or attractive. A famous psychologist noted, "If this civilization is ever buried by atomic holocaust, future anthropologists who resurrect the video tapes of major network commercials are certain to conclude that as a society we were offensive to each other in a degree never before reached on earth."[11] "Bad breath, body odor, loose dentures, psoriasis, warts, gastritis, hemorrhoids, feminine freshness, and foot odor constitute only a partial list of television advertising's critical concerns."[12] In essence, advertising convinces us - - sometimes even brainwashes us - - to believe these should be our critical concerns as well. (As an interesting side note, the field of advertising was created by John Watson who is the founding theorist of behavioral psychology).

Many of us are wise enough not to fall for these various kinds of advertised gimmicks. Nevertheless, very few of us are able to escape the subliminal messages and seductive entrapments of advertising which repeatedly convey the message that we are unacceptable as we are. In short, advertising persuades us that self-improvement can always be made - - and *should* be made.

Additionally, technology and science advances at such a rapid pace that products and services are continuously becoming newer and improved. Consequently, we also feel a compelling need to keep advancing with the newer and improved. In short, we want to maintain our status, our prestige, our power, and our physical attractiveness - - all those things that make us feel we have a rightful place high up on the social hierarchy. This is why we get facelifts at fifty, buy corvettes at sixty, and resist retirement at seventy. This drive to maintain the status quo is, for many people, a defense against getting old, which may explain our society's disturbing annoyance, avoidance and even mistreatment of the elderly. They mirror a fate which cannot be denied or escaped - - a fate which makes us feel helpless and inferior deep down in the core of our being.

Feelings of inferiority often serve as a springboard to ambition, success, and/or the desire for self-improvement which are not only admirable qualities but are essential to emotional health. In fact, most psychologists firmly believe the drive for self-fulfillment and personal achievement is paramount to our self-esteem and personal happiness. However, our drive can become a serious problem if our idea of what we could be, or what we should be, is unrealistic or unattainable.

Some individuals are so critical of themselves and judge themselves so harshly they begin to feel some degree of self-contempt that negatively affects their lives for many years without their understanding. Research consistently shows that both men and women judge themselves most harshly regarding their appearance and intelligence; therefore, these two traits are the most common sources for self-criticism.[13] Karen Horney, another prominent theorist, believed a person may begin to feel some measure of self-hate when he begins to realize that he cannot live up to the unrealistic high standards he has set for himself - - as no one can.[14] Any measure of self-hate signifies there is a war on - - he is at war with himself.[15]

I shall succumb, destroyed by myself
I who am two, what I could be and what I am.
And in the end one will annihilate the other…
(Christian Morgenstern, 1921)

Karen Horney believed the poet's reference to "what I could be" refers to the striving after an idealized self and becoming an ideal person.[16] This inner battle between the real self and the ideal self can be much worse for some than others. It is worse for those individuals who not only strive to fit in and belong but who also feel a compelling need to rise to the top and excel above all others. Some of these individuals have set goals for themselves that are so high they are doomed to fail, and when they do they suffer severe emotional consequences.

There is nothing wrong with striving for self-improvement or trying to fulfill the expectations of others and/or achieving extraordinary success, as long as we do so in keeping with the uniqueness of our individuality and the inherent qualities of our real selves. If, on the other hand, we believe we cannot accomplish these tasks unless we become someone other than who we really are, then a battle within can occur. The "what I am" can never be good enough or measure up to the "what I could be" or what I pretend to be, or what I hope to be. Famous people, such as movie stars and models, should be aware of this inner psychological battle since their fame and stardom - - as well as the public's idolization of them - - is primarily based on the creation and promotion of an idealized image.

When we unrealistically strive after an idealized self, we are bound to possess an extremely distorted and negative view of ourselves as we really are,[17] consequently, the real self can get lost under and/or persecuted by the idealized self, that is, the individual that we want to be. The real self becomes an offensive stranger to whom the idealized self happens to be attached and the latter turns against this stranger with hate and contempt for embarrassing him.[18]

> *Briefly, when an individual shifts his center of gravity to his idealized self, he not only exalts himself but also is bound to look at his actual self... from a wrong perspective. The glorified self becomes not only a phantom to be pursued; it also becomes a measuring rod with which to measure his actual being. And this actual being is an embarrassing sight when viewed from the perspective of godlike perfection that he cannot help but despise it. Moreover, what is dynamically more important, the human being which he actually is keeps interfering – significantly - with his flight to glory, and therefore he is bound to hate it, to hate himself. (Karen Horney, 1950, pp.110-111)*

We learn very early in life that we should not only hide any feelings we may have of self-contempt but we should also feel guilt and shame for having them. Nevertheless, some of us still feel these emotions deep down inside, but we cannot openly discuss them with anyone because they are socially unacceptable and frightening - - to ourselves as well as to others. However, as Sigmund Freud noted, any feeling that is denied or repressed will find expression in one way or another.[19] Karen Horney believed that self-contempt is often expressed through relentless demands on one's self, along with self- blame, self-tormenting, and self-destructive acts[20] such as overindulgence in substance abuse, hectic work schedules, illegal activities, sexual promiscuity, eating disorders, etc. etc.

In order to change, a person must examine the demands he makes on himself and realize they will eventually wear him down, both psychologically and physically. The bottom line is this question: Does he want to cease and retreat from this war within or is he destined to die in the battle? In other words, can he accept himself as a human being with all the general limitations and imperfections this implies but also with the possibility of his personal growth and happiness?[21] He must decide if he wants to continue to live the rest of his life in search of that which will fulfill his ideal self or for that which will fulfill his real self, since they can be at great odds with each other.[22]

In summary, because of our lifelong struggle to adapt, fit in, and belong, many of us develop an emotional security blanket that centers on perfection, superiority, and power, all of which facilitate the illusion of self-esteem and ego strength but does very little, if anything, to comfort our real selves. A famous theorist by the name of Alfred Adler believed that we feel inferior by our very nature because we are the only animal that is born "insufficient".[23] In other words, unlike other animals, we must create and produce the advantages and assets that will aid our survival and ensure our success.[24] Therefore, he believed it is every person's goal (consciously or unconsciously) to overcome his or her feelings of inferiority.[25] Therefore, the desire for perfection, superiority, and power are inherent in our nature because they help us to better adapt and survive in our external man-made world.[26]

Moreover, the pursuit of perfection, superiority, and power can be extremely enticing and seductive because it not only helps us to overcome our feelings of inferiority but is also a great distraction against just being still and living in the present moment. Being still gives us more opportunity to feel our separateness and aloneness and to question the meaning of our lives. This self-confrontation can be very difficult and can disturb even the psychologically strong.

Erich Fromm stated, *"Things have no self and men who have become things have no self."*[27] He believed man has been transformed into a "thing" so he is now plagued with anxiety as he lives without faith, conviction, and love; therefore, he must escape into empty "busy-ness".[28] However, we can only find fulfillment if we remain in touch with the fundamental facts of our existence, that is, if we can experience love and unity as well as aloneness.[29] If we are completely enmeshed in the routine of life and empty busy-ness, then we cannot see anything but our external man-made world.[30]

Recently, many authors have strongly advocated turning inward as the answer to personal happiness and it has been marketed like a "prescription for inner peace". Our current need to escape from the routine hustle and bustle of life is so crucial that we must now artificially incorporate moments of peace and tranquility into our hectic schedules through various pre-planned activities such as meditation, yoga, massages, happy hour, etc. These moments no longer occur spontaneously as they should because we are submerged in the chaos of daily living. It is not enough to create these moments of peace and tranquility in our lives - - we must also feel them. We must not only be able to stop and stand still but we must also be able to listen to our own heartfelt desires when there is silence. What good does it do to drown out our external world if we are alienated from our internal world, that is, if when we are alone we feel empty?

> *When they do attain more money, more distinction, more power, they also come to feel the whole impact of the futility of their chase. They do not secure any more peace of mind, inner security, or joy of living. The inner distress... is still as great as ever.... It is so deeply ingrained in all of us that everybody wants to get*

ahead of the next fellow, and be better than he is, that we feel these tendencies to be "natural." But the fact that compulsive drives for success will arise only in a competitive culture does not make them any less neurotic. Even in a competitive culture there are many people for whom other values – such as, in particular, that of growth as a human being – are more important than competitive excelling over others. (Karen Horney, 1950, p.26)

The strong advocacy of turning inward as a prescription for inner peace recognizes that inner peace and tranquility are not products that are purchased or created by another but rather must be discovered by each person within himself or herself. The proponents of this advocacy however fail to acknowledge how much work and courage this discovery requires. Introspective work can be a difficult prospect because we must drown out all the noise and interference from our external world, and turn our focus inward. Sometimes the prospect of looking inward can be frightening, and this is the precise reason why some of us continuously carry painful emotional baggage day in and day out. We think it is easier to endure the weight of these burdens rather than to face them, come to terms with them, and let them go.

Authentic self-esteem and inner peace can only emerge when there is congruence between what is real within us and what is ideal, that is, what we really are and what we think we should be. An essential first step toward achieving this congruence is to identify our beliefs. Because our beliefs are more conscious than our feelings, our beliefs are the more retrievable aspects of our personalities. In other words, it is easier to make conscious that which we think versus that which we feel. Examining the beliefs we have about ourselves, others, and the world in which we live is the essential first step to a better understanding of ourselves, for our beliefs are the by-product of all our learning and life experiences. Our beliefs, whether self-imposed or imposed by our society, shaped and molded our personalities in childhood, therefore, they laid the groundwork for the self-esteem and self-image we have as adults.

Therapy may provide the best arena in which these complex emotions can be examined - - but it is not the only arena. There is a vast variety of self-help material available to anyone seeking to better understand himself or herself. No matter what arena we choose, the ultimate key to finding our real selves is to begin looking - - to open the door to the past and search for the time when our real self was present and whole. When we can identify that time, we can more easily trace the events that followed to understand when, where, and why we embarked on a path to a pseudo reality and a pseudo self.

In conclusion, we cannot ignore our real self because it is our real self that cries out to be known, understood, and loved. There can be no true inner peace and contentment if a person ignores his real self, that is, if he ignores his genuine emotions and the true yearnings within his heart.

CHAPTER 2
KNOW THYSELF

"Illusions about oneself can become crutches useful to those who are not able to walk alone; but they increase a person's weakness..."Know thyself" is one of the fundamental commands that aim at human strength and happiness." (Erich Fromm)

Every person needs awareness and understanding of his real self from which all else emerges, and those who lack this core self-knowledge spend a lifetime often feeling estranged from themselves. Although we have a basic need to know ourselves, this need can be thwarted very early in childhood by family, and/or in adulthood by society; nevertheless, this basic need for self-knowledge still exists. No other kind of knowledge is more essential to emotional health than self-knowledge, yet so many individuals live their lives without it. They search the world over for answers when the answers they seek lie within themselves.

Our past reveals how and why we have become who we are. Some psychologists believe an individual's personality and self-image are fully formed in early childhood. One famous psychologist theorized that before we are eight years old we not only form a concept about our own self-worth but we also formulate a concept about the worth of others.[1] He believed that our sense of self-worth is dependent upon having our emotional needs met in early childhood. If we received support, affection, attention, and praise, then we developed a core belief that "I'm okay".[2] If our emotional needs were not met in childhood, that is, if we were neglected, teased, abandoned, or abused, then we developed a core belief that "I'm not okay".[3] In short, our parents or caretakers, through their own capacity to love, and through praise and punishment, shaped and molded our self-concept, either positively or negatively.

The negative self-concept that some of us developed in childhood was emotionally painful and damaging, not only because our true self was rejected but because the rejection came from those whom we loved and who were supposed to love us.[4] Through their actions or inactions we learned how lovable or unlovable we are, and what we learned became ingrained in our unconscious minds. Learning that we are unlovable, although emotionally painful, is fairly easy. Unlearning it is extremely difficult.

We have a basic emotional need to love and to be loved and all that occurred in our childhood will significantly impact our ability to fulfill this need in adulthood. Ideally, as children, we should have felt and believed we were lovable, as this feeling is crucial for healthy emotional survival. The feeling of being loved, and even more importantly, of being lovable, is perhaps one of the greatest values and sources of contentment in life.[5] Conversely, the feeling of not being lovable can be a source of profound distress.[6] If we did not feel lovable in childhood, we will not feel lovable as adults; and we will do whatever we perceive as necessary to compensate for this deficit as well as whatever is necessary to block these painful feelings from our conscious awareness.

When we are made to feel unlovable, inferior, or inadequate in childhood, we grow up believing that we must conceal who we really are because we have learned that who we really are is unacceptable.[7] In other words, we were not only rejected by those who were supposed to love us but we compound the injury further by rejecting ourselves. Gradually we become disconnected from our real thoughts and feelings so that we can become that which we think we are supposed to be - - that which ensures we will be esteemed, accepted, and loved.[8]

This disconnection from our real thoughts and feelings sets the stage for the development of a false self and further estrangement from who we are as unique individuals.

Through a variety of adverse influences, a child may not be permitted to grow according to his individual needs and possibilities. Such unfavorable circumstances are too manifold to list here. But, when summarized, they all boil down to the fact that the people in his environment are too wrapped up in their own neuroses to be able to love the child, or even to conceive of him as the particular individual he is; their attitudes toward him are determined by their own neurotic needs and responses. In simple words, they may be dominating, overprotective, intimidating, irritable, over-exacting, overindulgent, erratic, partial to other siblings, hypocritical, indifferent, etc. It is never a matter of just a single factor, but always the whole constellation that exerts untoward influence on a child's growth. As a result, the child does not develop a feeling of belonging, of "we", but a profound insecurity and vague apprehensiveness, ... It is his feeling of being isolated and helpless in a world conceived of as potentially hostile... For many reasons, he has not had the chance to develop real self confidence: his inner strength has been sapped by his having to be on the defensive, by his being divided...Hence he desperately needs self confidence, or a substitute for it.... If he had a sense of belonging, his feeling inferior to others would not be so serious a handicap. But living in a competitive society, and feeling at bottom — as he does — he can only develop an urgent need to lift himself above others.... Gradually and unconsciously, the imagination sets to work and creates in his mind an idealized image of himself..... And this idealized self becomes more real to him than his real self..... It is a curious and exclusively human process. It would hardly occur to a cocker spaniel that he is "really" an Irish setter. (Karen Horney, 1950, pp.18, 20 -23)

The creation in our minds of an idealized image (or a false self) can be related to Darwin's concept of *"survival of the fittest"*. In other words, we must not only physically adapt to our environment but we must also psychologically adapt because feelings of endangerment come not only from physical threats, but, more often, from perceived psychological threats -- threats to our self-esteem and personal dignity, such as being rejected, or being treated unjustly or rudely, or being insulted or demeaned. [9] In order to ward off these threats and emotionally survive in this world, many individuals develop an idealized image that not only serves as an emotional form of protective armor but also provides the self-esteem the individual needs to feel some degree of inner confidence and emotional security. However, real self-esteem cannot come from an idealized image or a false self. It can only come from the real self, and the real self can only come from acquiring self-knowledge -- from following the fundamental command that aims at human strength and happiness, that is, "know thyself".

Many pop psychology authors emphasize the attainment of self-esteem as opposed to the attainment of self-knowledge. They talk about the subject of self-esteem as if it were one inherent static quality that we possess or that we do not possess. As a famous psychologist noted, no other term is used more in connection with psychology than self-esteem, yet, little attention has been given to actually defining what it is, the reasons why we need it, the conditions we must satisfy to achieve it, and its relationship to our emotional well-being and personal happiness.[10]

Self-esteem is generally conceived of as a positive feeling of well-being or a satisfying appraisal of oneself. Over the course of a lifetime, however, our self-esteem can fluctuate because various life events can impact, undermine, and even change it - - for better or for worse. It would probably be more accurate to substitute the term "self-esteem" with the term "psychological health" because the criterion that defines psychological health is far more constant and stable. Many renowned psychologists have proven this point without dispute. They do not focus on the attainment of self-esteem per se but rather on the attainment of self-knowledge. To ignore or replace their theories and wisdom would be scoffing at genius.

Moreover, in many ways, what constitutes self-esteem for one person may be very different for another. Some people derive their self-esteem simply from being loved. Others derive a sense of self-esteem by being capable in those particular skills and activities which he or she personally values the most. However, some people, although capable in certain particular skills, may still have deep feelings of inferiority and still lack self-esteem because although they are highly accomplished in certain areas, they may not feel capable or adequate in those particular skills and activities which they value most in life.

A prominent psychologist believed that our need for self-esteem is inherent in our nature however we are not born with the knowledge of what will satisfy this need - - we must discover it within ourselves.[11] In other words, every person has a need to feel good about himself, but he is uncertain as to what will make him feel it consistently and authentically.

Man experiences his desire for self-esteem as an urgent imperative, as a basic need...He cannot escape the feeling that his estimate of himself is of life and death importance...So intensely does a man feel the need of a positive view of himself, that he may evade, repress, and distort his judgment, disintegrate his mind - in order to avoid coming face to face with facts that would affect his self appraisal adversely... If and to the extent that men lack self-esteem, they feel driven to fake it, to create the illusion of self-esteem — condemning themselves to chronic psychological fraud. (Nathaniel Branden, 1969, p.110)

Self-knowledge liberates us from the need to commit psychological fraud providing that we also acquire self-acceptance. In short, if we can accept all that is real within us, the good and the bad, the painful and the pleasant, our genuine likes and dislikes, etc., then we know who we are and with absolute certainty we know that which distinguishes "you" from "me". It is this self-knowledge which provides us with the essential foundation to build from, to grow from, and to love from. When we fully know and accept ourselves as we really are, we then have no need to invest our energy in creating an illusion of self-esteem. When we know and accept who we really are, authentic self-esteem will emerge and flourish. In essence, self-esteem is the by-product of self-knowledge rather than the goal.

If we are to become real, alive, and integrated, we must get in touch with all our true feelings no matter how painful or unpleasant. When we deny our true feelings for a long period of time, we become disconnected from ourselves and often behave in ways we do not understand. Moreover, our true emotions can become so entangled that we no longer know what we are really feeling or why we feel it. This emotional entanglement can cause inner turmoil which presses for release and may be manifested in unexplainable and uncontrollable emotional outbursts - - outbursts that reveal how entangled our emotions have become as we feel a mixture of anger, sadness, fear, and helplessness all at the same time. In essence, our emotions have become intertwined. They are no longer separate and pure like they were when we were children.

In short, if we do not understand what we feel and why we feel it, then we do not know who we really are. We are disconnected from our real selves and our real problems. We are strangers to ourselves.

> *The loss of self is a "sickness unto death" ...it is a despair which does not clamor or scream ... Any other loss – that of a job say, or a leg – arouses far more concern.... Patients coming for consultation complain about headaches, sexual disturbances, inhibitions in work, or other symptoms: as a rule they do not complain about having lost touch with the core of their psychic existence. (Soren Kierkegaard, 1941)*

Physicians are often overburdened with patients who present a host of physical complaints (real and imagined) because of underlying and unknown psychological difficulties. It has been asserted that more than seventy percent of visits to the doctor's office are not based on any real physical problems but rather are purely psychological.

Acquiring self-knowledge depends upon our ability to be introspective and honest with ourselves. Although we may want to understand ourselves better, our defense mechanisms protect us from the emotional discomfort this introspective work requires. In other words, our need to know ourselves may be in great conflict with our need to protect ourselves from that same knowledge. Although, we have a basic need to know, sometimes we also have a need not to know.[12]

As Sigmund Freud noted, whenever we seek knowledge about ourselves, we often confront our own resistance; therefore, self-knowledge can be the most difficult kind of knowledge to attain. [13]

> *More than any other knowledge we fear knowledge of ourselves, knowledge that might transform our self-esteem and our self-image... While human beings love knowledge and seek it – they are curious – they also fear it. The closer to the personal it is, the more they fear it. (Abraham Maslow, 1966, p.16)*

Sigmund Freud was the first to talk about our fear of self-knowledge, and he spoke in depth about our use of unconscious defense mechanisms to keep unpleasant or painful memories from our conscious awareness.[14] Simultaneously, some defense mechanisms are necessary, otherwise we would be overwhelmed with too much emotional pain. For these reasons, when we want to acquire a better understanding of ourselves, professional help may be necessary.

An essential goal of therapy is to help an individual feel less defensive so that his or her real problems can surface and be resolved. In essence, the therapist helps him to feel safe rather than guarded or afraid as he discovers who he really is. The therapist accompanies and protects him as he goes on a mental exploration and journey into his past, especially back to his childhood, because the negative evaluations he made about himself in childhood are often unfair, unrealistic, and irrational.

As children, we were not able to logically rationalize why certain events happened as they did.[15] As children, we were egocentric so we viewed the world as revolving totally around ourselves. [16] This very limited perspective caused us to blame ourselves for every bad thing that happened for, as children, we could not hypothesize any other explanation.[17] Because of these intellectual limitations in childhood, we internalized and personalized our unhappy circumstances as somehow being our fault and therefore true reflections of our worth and lovableness.

In childhood, we concluded, "It is because of me, I am unlovable" or "I am inadequate" but as adults, we can go back and reevaluate these childhood events and circumstances. We can now examine the many factors outside of ourselves that have nothing to do with who we were. When we do, we will discover that the inadequacies were in our caretakers, or in their circumstances, but not within us. We will realize it was because of *their* inadequacies and not ours that we did not have the nurturing environment we needed to foster our healthy emotional development.

> *The human individual, given a chance... will develop the unique alive forces of his real self: the clarity and depth of his own feelings, thoughts, wishes, interests; the ability to tap his own resources, the strength of his will power; the special capacities or gifts he may have; the faculty to express himself, and to relate himself to others with his spontaneous feelings. All this will in time enable him to find his set of values and his aims in life... But, like any other living organism, the human individual needs favorable conditions for his growth... he needs an atmosphere of warmth to give him both a feeling of inner security and the inner freedom enabling him to have his own feelings and thoughts and to express himself. He needs the good will of others, not only to help him in his many needs but to guide him and encourage him to become a mature and fulfilled individual (Karen Horney, 1950, pp.17-18)*

If we want to better understand ourselves, we need to examine the circumstances we had when we were children. Were they favorable circumstances for our growth? Did we have an atmosphere of warmth to give us a feeling of inner security and a feeling of inner freedom? Did we have the good will of others to guide us and encourage us to become mature, contented, and fulfilled individuals? We should have had all this in our home environment and those of us who did not embarked on life's journey emotionally unprepared to deal with life's difficulties - - to deal with dysfunctional people, a complex society, and a troubled world.

The challenge we have before us is to find the courage to open the door to our past and start gaining a complete understanding of ourselves. This courage can come from logic and reason for although we cannot control what we feel, we can control what we think. Reason may be a very small voice but it is the beginning of a cure. As we journey back to our childhood recalling painful events, logic and reason will tell us some things with absolute certainty - - one being that we were just children, and as children we should have been loved, protected, and cared for by our parents. From this premise, on which no one could possibly disagree, we must then ask, "Why"? Why were we not loved and cared for the way we should have been? When we ask ourselves this question, we open a floodgate of memories that may be emotionally painful but ultimately rewarding, because, for the first time in our lives, we can begin to see things in the right perspective.

When we look back into our childhood we begin to recall all the events that impacted and shaped our self-concept and feelings of self-worth. We begin to see that the inadequacies were in our caretakers, or in their circumstances, and *not* within us. We begin to realize that the fact that we were not loved did not mean we were not lovable. We begin to see ourselves as innocent children who should not have been neglected nor mistreated - - who should have been loved and cared for - - who were not at fault for anything except, perhaps, being born into a dysfunctional family. When we look at ourselves in this light we will come to embrace the child within us and begin the venture of personality integration and total self-acceptance. The need for a false self will dissipate because authentic self-esteem can now emerge and flourish, along with a sense of security, contentment and inner peace.

***

The following is an exercise that was given to group members in order to help them journey back into their past. They were asked to, "Get out a family album or pictures of yourself as a child. Let your memories emerge. Were these happy times? Sad times? Serious times? What thoughts and feelings are evoked? What does this child believe about herself or himself"?

***

"What does this child believe about herself? This child believes it was unloved and was an ugly duckling ... born unattractive and awkward in a fancy and sophisticated world." Susan K.

————

"When I look back at some childhood pictures, I realize I look scared and serious. The best I can recall is that these were very sad times for me. I was the middle child and I was jealous of both my older and younger sister because I felt like she loved them more than me. I felt like my mother was in another world. She didn't show any feelings. I felt left out all the time. My father was drunk a lot and my mother was always busy trying to please him and keep the peace. I suppose I learned to withdraw very early in life when I was hurt so many times from being rejected by them. I started isolating and keeping to myself so I wouldn't get hurt anymore." Betty J.

———

" I really don't have a lot of childhood memories. My mom was the one who always corrected me. I do remember getting quite a few slaps on the fanny with a paddle. I don't remember either parent being very affectionate with kisses or hugs. When I think back on my childhood, the unpleasant feelings that are aroused in me are being afraid, feeling alone, and feeling angry and funny enough, I still feel like this today." Linda G.

———

"Whenever I think of my childhood, I see my mother coming in my room after the bars had closed and calling me every name in the book she could think of and my dad would pretend to be sleeping and never once came to my defense. My younger sister had her own room next to mine but not once did my mother open her door in the middle of the night and curse her out. This made me believe even more that they resented me for being born. My mother and father were very young when I was conceived and they "had to get married". Many times, even during my most vulnerable moments, this was thrown in my face that I ruined my mother's life. So I was supposed to feel fortunate that they "gave up their lives" so I could be born. No one ever told me they loved me or hugged me and I was such an affectionate child. I have always blamed myself for their inability to love me." Anna H.

"When I look at our childhood pictures, I wonder is there an individual there? There is still a lot of that little girl in me today. I was a good kid. I was afraid to be a bad kid. My mother had a temper - - not often, but I guess it would build. She used to chase me up the steps and threaten physical harm. I remember my sisters at the top of the stairs and they were scared too. I was one of three girls and we were always referred to "as 'the girls". When someone leaves me I feel like that little girl. I feel the terror and abandonment I felt as a kid especially when my father got sick and had to be hospitalized. I was afraid to do anything to set my father off and send him back to the hospital. I believed I was responsible for other people's reactions so I always tried to be a pleaser. My identity was always hidden while I tried not to make people angry - - tried to smooth things over and keep things calm. Somehow I was always afraid to be myself - - what if no one liked me? Then I started forgetting who I was in the first place. No wonder I feel so lost sometimes." Nancy B.

CHAPTER 3
EMOTIONAL PAIN AND SORROW

"The existence of contemporary people is marked by aloneness, fear, and bewilderment." (Erich Fromm)

Many people feel unhappy without knowing why; therefore, they cannot articulate the reasons for their unhappiness in any concrete or meaningful way. This phenomenon occurs in part because our society teaches us to conceal our unhappiness and emotional pain, and as a result, some individuals become adept at not only denying these emotions from others but also from themselves.

Additionally, it is sometimes difficult to understand the emotional pain we experience in our own personal lives, and it is even more difficult to comprehend the pain and suffering we see in the world around us. In fact, the profound degree of suffering we are exposed to in today's society - - violence, terrorism, war, world hunger, homelessness, etc. - - can be so overwhelming and perplexing that we often feel the need to run for cover or emotionally shut down. In other words, sometimes we must stick our heads in the sand in order to emotionally survive because as human beings with limited resources, both psychologically and financially, we cannot possibly assist all the needy people and worthy causes in the world. So in order to better cope with our disturbing reality and preserve our emotional well being, we tend to adopt a "survival of the fittest" mentality, that is, those who are strong and can help themselves will survive and those who cannot will perish.

Although it is becoming increasingly more difficult to comprehend much of the suffering in the world around us, it is not so difficult to understand the suffering we experience in our own lives. As human beings, we cannot avoid experiences that cause emotional pain and sorrow for they are an expected part of every person's life:

> *A person who is alive and sensitive cannot fail to be sad, and to feel sorrow many times in his life. This is so, not only because of the amount of unnecessary suffering produced by the imperfection of our social arrangements, but because of the nature of human existence which makes it impossible not to react to life with a good deal of pain and sorrow. Since we are living beings, we must be sadly aware of the necessary gap between our aspirations and what can be achieved in our short and troubled life. Since death confronts us with the inevitable fact that either we shall die before our loved ones or they before us – since we see suffering, the unavoidable as well as the unnecessary…how can we avoid the experience of pain and sorrow? The effort to avoid it is only possible if we reduce our sensitivity, responsiveness, and love, if we harden our hearts and withdraw our attention and our feelings from others, as well as from ourselves. (Erich Fromm, 1955, p. 201)*

The emotional pain and sorrow we experience can help us to acquire a deeper understanding of ourselves. Moreover, it is our trials and tribulations, that is, the mountains we had to climb and the milestones we had to overcome, that tell the real story about who we are as unique individuals. Psychologists know that only after they understand the nature and degree of a person's unhappiness, that which has caused him the deepest emotional pain, only then will they begin to fully understand the person and how he came to be the way he is today.

The emotional pain an individual experiences from loss, separation, betrayal, rejection, injustice, death of a loved one, etc. becomes an integrated part of his personality and an inseparable part of his being. Moreover, the nature and degree of his pain can significantly alter the path the rest of his life will take.

In today's society, many people tend to view their emotional pain as a personal detriment which provides nothing meaningful to be learned or gained. They do not make any attempt to analyze their pain because they do not realize the importance of fully understanding the underlying causes. They do not realize their unhappiness may be a signal to change themselves or their lives. Moreover, a careful self-examination of one's emotional pain can unlock the door to the unconscious mind and provide an individual with invaluable self-knowledge and inner strength. But, instead, some individuals tend to perceive their pain as a setback, as punishment, or as personal failure, so they believe they will be shamed or shunned by others if they expose it.

Viktor Frankl, a renowned psychologist, theorized that the personal suffering an individual experiences in his lifetime may not be a sign of personal failure or abnormality but rather it may be a sign of personal achievement, particularly if his suffering is a result of his search for meaning in his life.[1] A man's concern, even his despair, over the worth of his life is an existential distress but by no means a mental disorder.[2]

Some individuals are carrying a lifetime of accumulated hurts and losses and, consequently, they spend a great deal of mental energy repressing the hurt they feel. Because all emotional pain cuts to the core of our essence - - that is, it assaults who we really are underneath the surface - - we feel the need to repress, deny, or conceal our pain in order to emotionally survive and function normally again, but repressed pain never loses its grip on us. It forever controls and dictates our behavior and influences our entire being in very powerful ways. As an unknown author explained, un-grieved losses remain forever alive in our unconscious minds for the unconscious mind has no sense of time. Past losses and separations impact our current ability to love and form future attachments; therefore, it is essential to identify un-grieved losses because identifying them is the beginning of breaking free from the painful hold they have on us.

For most of us, the use of repression started very early in childhood when we were first unable to make sense of our reality or our circumstances:

> *The encounter with human irrationality, in childhood, is one of the earliest psychological traumas in the lives of many people, and one of the earliest occasions of repression. At a time when a young mind is struggling to acquire a firm grasp of reality, it is often confronted - through the actions of parents and other adults - with what appears to be an incomprehensible universe. It is not inanimate objects which appear incomprehensible, but people. It is not nature that appears threatening, but human beings. And, more often then not, the problem is submerged by him or her, repressed, ignored, never dealt with, never understood, never conquered. (Nathaniel Branden, 1969, p.90)*

In some instances, repressed emotional pain becomes manifest in anger, especially if we have been badly victimized and/or have suffered a painful betrayal, injustice or loss. Our anger comes from a sense of pressure to do something to help ourselves, yet many times, we can do nothing [3] and not being able to do anything to defend, avenge, or help ourselves only further exacerbates our anger. As a notable psychologist explained, anger is primarily a reaction to feelings of helplessness - - intense anger may produce a fleeting feeling of power that combats the feeling of helplessness.[4]

Anger can be a difficult emotion to experience because it is generally an unacceptable emotion to display in public; therefore, individuals are often uncomfortable with their feelings of anger. The following are responses from clients regarding their anger. The names noted are fictitious:

***

"If I started to feel my anger, I feel I would sink into a horrible depression. I think I would start to feel sorry for myself and become absolutely miserable with my life. I have always believed anger is wrong, anger was not good for you, and certainly not acceptable behavior." Joan G.

———

"I feel very guilty when anger comes over me because I sometimes throw things when I lose my temper but my pattern for how I handle my anger has changed a lot. Now I talk to someone about it and get it out. Sometimes I even cry because it makes me feel better. Holding the anger in is not good for me and I now know it is okay to get angry." Sue M.

——

"I have always been afraid of anger. I relate anger to when I was growing up and my parents would argue. I associate anger with fear and abandonment. My mother would always express her anger toward my father - - yell at him and make him feel small - - and for years I never expressed my own anger because I never wanted to be like my mother." Karen L.

———

"If I really started to feel my anger I would probably become overwhelmed and cry. I feel anger is ugly and nobody likes you if you are angry. As a child, I learned to cover my anger and just smile all the time in spite of how I was really feeling inside." Donna P.

———

"When I start to get angry, I am usually concerned about what the other person might think or feel if I express it. I feel scared too because deep down inside I feel anger is not okay. It was never acceptable to show anger while growing up. If I did, I was told I was a bad person. Whenever I get angry as an adult I tend to feel afraid." Chris J.

———

"I am afraid of my anger therefore I usually keep it to myself and then unexpectedly explode after an upsetting event. I believe my anger will make people dislike me or not want to be with me and this is why I try to hide it." Tom B.

———

"If I started to feel my anger, I would probably feel better and less depressed. If I let my anger out at appropriate times, it would not have a chance to build up and explode. I would learn that it was safe to express anger and that people don't go away - - afterwards you can still have a good relationship with them. But deep inside I have always believed anger would make people go away. I thought it would make people not love me so I always got hurt instead of angry. I have always turned my anger inward on myself and spent a great deal of time being depressed as an adult. Most of my life I've tried to avoid conflicts and keep relationships harmonious – all at the expense of losing a part of who I was." Lisa G.

———

"I always show my anger way too much. It is a bad habit that I wish I didn't have. When I was younger, I let people walk all over me, but in the past five years I have gone to the complete opposite way of responding. Deep inside I believe everyone in the world gets angry but not to the extent that I do." Dan S.

———

"My anger really scares me sometimes. How can you be fifty years old and not have many things to be angry about? Sometimes I feel that if I allowed myself to get as angry as I could be - - or I should be - - I might lose my mind or, worse than that, maybe do something crazy." Steve C.

***

Anger that is justifiable with no legitimate recourse or outlet eventually leads to bitterness and cynicism because we must not only recover from the profound hurt and loss but we must also recover from the assault we have suffered to our personal dignity. In these situations, rigorous physical exercise can be a good outlet. Without a constructive outlet, we may find ourselves vacillating between profound anger and sadness. In short, when we are not angry we are deeply unhappy which cannot be easily hidden from ourselves or from others. Eventually the sorrow comes to live in our eyes.[5]

Experiences which cause us profound emotional pain can dramatically change us for better or for worse, but we can choose *how* we will be changed. Making this choice empowers us and ultimately makes us stronger:

> *The way in which a man accepts his fate and all the suffering it entails, the way in which he takes up his cross, gives him ample opportunity - even under the most difficult circumstances - to add a deeper meaning to his life. He may remain brave, dignified, and unselfish or in the bitter fight for self-preservation he may forget his human dignity and become no more than an animal. Here lies the chance for a man either to make use of or forgo the opportunities of attaining the moral values that a difficult situation may afford him. (Viktor Frankl, 1959, p.88)*

The specific way in which we "take up our cross" or endure our emotional pain is sometimes the only meaning we will ever derive from some experiences, especially if we have suffered a senseless or incomprehensible tragedy, betrayal, or injustice.

When personal tragedy, betrayal, or injustice strikes we are thrust into a new and painful reality. The word "strikes" is purposefully used because this word describes the way in which these events usually occur, that is, very suddenly and without warning. This suddenness makes the event that much harder to handle because we are shocked into a new reality for which we have had no time to mentally process or prepare. Therefore, after an emotionally traumatic event, we may obsessively think about what has happened to us in order to somehow make sense of our new reality and exert some control over it.

The more difficult it is to make sense of what has happened to us, the more we may obsess about it. If we can begin to understand why this bad thing has happened, then we can begin to reduce our feelings of helplessness and regain our emotional balance. Initially, this kind of obsessive thinking can be emotionally healthy if it helps us to somehow understand and work through our feelings of grief, pain, and loss; however, some suffering we incur will *never* make sense and we will never comprehend it no matter how much we may think about it.

When we have experienced a human cruelty such as tragedy, betrayal, or injustice, we not only feel profound anger and hurt but we may also feel victimized. These thoughts and feelings are tremendously powerful because they cause us to feel "flooded" and out of control, which can be emotionally overwhelming and distressful.[6]

This feeling of being flooded by emotional distress may be likened to the fight/flight syndrome which is an outdated survival mechanism that we have inherited from our ancestors. In other words, whenever we feel physically or emotionally threatened, our bodies prepare in various ways to ward off this threat. Therefore, when we are victimized, we feel threatened and we react involuntarily by wanting to strike back (fight) or run away and escape (flight).[7] However, unlike our primitive ancestors, we are rarely able to strike back or run away because our threatening stimuli are now more psychological rather than physical. This is why we currently experience so much stress and strain in our lives. We can neither fight nor escape the threatening stimuli or stressors that confront us. We must instead remain passive and endure them.

It is important to understand that "flooding" causes us to become overwhelmed by inescapable and out of control emotions in which we become helplessly fixated or stuck, and this fixation can wear us down both psychologically and physically.[8] If we relive a painful event over and over again with intense emotions and we are trapped in this repetitive cycle, then this is a sure sign that we have been badly traumatized and/or emotionally wounded.

Once an individual has been traumatized and/or emotionally wounded, he is no longer the same person he was in the past.[9] He does not see himself, others, or the world around him in the same way he did before,[10] but if no one articulates this truth for him, he will remain confused, alone, and afraid. The journey back to normalcy is usually a long hard road and he will often stumble, fall, and even crawl as he tries to regain his emotional balance.

> *Once you have been traumatized, you live in a world that is different from that of other people.... What constitutes a traumatic experience is, to a degree, a subjective matter....If you feel personally damaged by the experience, then for you it was traumatic....Living with trauma takes on a whole new dimension of loneliness....You must not only contend with the terrible events that happened to you, but also the person you have become as a result of it....You realize that things have changed between you and others - you are no longer the same person you were before and you can't enjoy yourself with others in the same way.... It's like discovering you are defective and no longer a full fledge member of society.... You have a different view of the world and its dangers....You find it difficult to maintain illusions of security, because you know what could potentially happen. You are no longer able to maintain the belief that illness and bad things only happen to the "other guy".... Often illusions of security are lost altogether. (Don Catherall, 1992, pp.2-43)*

When you have been emotionally wounded, you must learn how to avoid becoming permanently stuck in emotional pain. You must work toward healing. You should never underestimate how important it is to work toward emotional healing because unhealed emotional wounds stay with you forever. As a notable psychologist observed, "human cruelties" are not easily forgotten, and it is the permanency of these memories which cause us to fear anything vaguely similar to the emotional assault we have suffered.[11]

The essential first step to emotional healing is telling your story to another person (e.g., a therapist, priest, or friend). No matter how independent you are, or how embarrassed or uncomfortable you may feel, you need to talk about what has happened to you. Moreover, each time you tell your story, you achieve some mastery and control over it, and eventually you are able to deal with the painful experience without becoming overwhelmed or broken by it. Once you have begun to face and eventually accept what has happened, you can then begin to mourn the loss of the way things used to be. The following disclosure by an anonymous client illustrates her pain and struggle to survive a traumatic life-altering experience.

***

"My daughter and I are alone now. We completely pulled away from our family a number of months ago. It was a painful decision but we just didn't want to be hurt anymore.

It started 15 years ago when my mother died and I questioned the missing assets in her estate. Everyone in my family knew I was totally justified in doing so, but two of my nephews didn't like it - - perhaps because they stood in direct line to inherit the missing assets I was questioning.

We ultimately resolved the issue - - not at all to my satisfaction - - but I felt we needed to end it once and for all and put it behind us. Had I known that my two disgruntled nephews had vengeance in their hearts and had no intentions of putting it behind them, I would never have resolved the issue the way I did. I would have, instead, taken it to court to have the missing assets (worth millions) taken out of the name they were in and placed into my mother's estate where they belonged.

My nephews severed their relationship with me and I have not seen or spoken to them since. It always amazed me how they could dismiss my daughter and me from their lives so easily. Did this speak to the shallowness of their feelings for us - - or just to their shallowness? But anyway, the rest of the family still loved us even though they accepted invitations to family functions knowing my daughter and I were neither invited nor welcomed. They were not concerned about it. They felt that it was none of their business.

I remember the first Christmas my daughter and I sat home alone while the whole family was celebrating together at my nephew's house. I foolishly believed that anyone with an ounce of sensitivity would realize how hurtful it must be to not have Christmas dinner with your family, not because you are sick, or had to work, or were out of town, but because you are not welcome. Surely, someone from the "loving" side of my family would call and express *something,* but nobody called except my loving sister. She called my daughter and told her about the wonderful day they all had and how they missed my brother because he was the only one not there.

Family get-togethers for Christmas, Thanksgiving, Easter, Weddings, Christenings etc. where my daughter and I were not invited, came and went and nobody had a word to say about it. It was a taboo subject. As the years rolled by it was clear that my daughter and I were no longer part of the family and it was more painfully clear that nobody cared.

Whenever we were together there was a whale in the room with us. Nobody would talk about it - - and I *needed* to talk about it. I needed them to explain how they could care anything about us and at the same time, go along with my nephews' decision to exclude us from the family. I needed to reconcile their love with their actions and I couldn't do it. They just didn't want to talk about it. The only comment they would ever make was that it is over and done with and I should put the past behind me. My daughter and I are not part of the family anymore - - that's not the past, but the present. How do we put the present behind us?

A few years ago, on an occasion when my daughter and I were with the "loving" side of our family, I seized the occasion as a rare opportunity to talk -- to tell them how, in the past few years, I had sleepless nights, severe headaches, and loss of hair over the family situation. In short, I spilled my guts all over the floor. I thought maybe they didn't care because they didn't know. I thought maybe if we had an honest dialogue, the whale would finally swim away and disappear. Frankly, I don't know what I thought. I later learned from my family that talking about my feelings on this occasion was very inappropriate - - and I agreed with that. It was not only inappropriate but totally pointless. I would like to think that I just had a moment of temporary insanity but I am afraid it was more in line with monumental stupidity. After my desperate disclosure of emotional pain, with the *only* response being, "it was inappropriate", I could no longer deny the painful truth. They went along with my nephews because, very simply, they didn't care that much for us - - if they cared anything at all. There was nothing to reconcile.

I will end the way I began. My daughter and I are alone now. We have completely pulled away from our family. The alienation is irreparable - - and believe it or not - - *they blame us for it.*

I think about my family now and then and wonder if any of them ever reflect back on what has happened with us. What do they think or feel about the decision my nephews made years ago to exclude my daughter and me from the family? And more importantly, what do they think or feel about the part they played in validating that decision? Now that they have the benefit of hindsight, do they see themselves as incredibly insensitive? uncaring? even cruel? I don't know the answers to these questions because they would never talk about it - - and now there's no longer any reason to talk about it. The whale is dead - - and dead whales don't swim." Susan Q.

***

Sometimes, emotional healing can only be accomplished in therapy. As a respected psychologist noted, the primary agenda in therapy is the integration of our experiences, traumatic or otherwise, into a renewed sense of self.[12] Additionally, if we have an artistic outlet into which our emotional pain can be channeled, then this more solitary release can also be helpful to our emotional healing. Sigmund Freud theorized the unconscious mind is highly receptive to symbolic meanings and messages that are conveyed through dreams, metaphors, stories, and art.[13] Therefore, like dreams, art may also be the *"royal road to the unconscious"*.[14] Similarly, as Somerset Maugham was known to believe, "the artist produces for the liberation of his soul."

Sometimes, in a desperate attempt to make sense of the event that caused our emotional pain, we blame ourselves.[15] We may begin to believe that we somehow caused or could have prevented this bad thing that happened to us.[16] This tendency to blame ourselves illustrates how powerful our intrinsic need is to make sense of reality. We have a basic need to believe that the world makes sense, "that there is a cause for every effect and a reason for everything that happens," so much so that we throw logic away in a desperate attempt to make sense of the senseless.[17] This self-blame is the worst possible blow we can give to ourselves.[18]

> *One of the worst things that happens to a person who has been hurt by life is that he tends to compound the damage by hurting himself a second time. Not only is he the victim of rejection, bereavement, injury, or bad luck; but he often feels the need to see himself as a bad person who had this coming to him and because of that drives away people who try to come close to him and help him. (Rabbi Kushner, 1981, p. 87)*

If we undeservingly blame ourselves for something bad that has happened to us, then we are most likely accustomed to putting ourselves down on a regular basis. This readiness to assume blame is directly related to feelings of low self-worth. So, at the very least, our self-blame reveals something about ourselves of which we may not have been previously aware. This new awareness is an example of how understanding our emotional pain can provide insight into our unconscious thoughts and feelings.

It is important to realize that betrayal, tragedy, injustice, or any other human cruelty is just a bad chapter in our lives -- and one bad chapter does not define us. We should not waste our lives being consumed by emotional pain, thus victimizing ourselves even further. For our emotional health and survival, *we must let it go,* but emotional healing can be a very difficult process. Getting past our pain and sorrow so that inner peace can emerge can be one of life's most difficult tasks because our pain can be so deep and consuming that it permeates every aspect of our lives. Our pain and sorrow can become an intangible burden which we carry everyday and from which we cannot break free. In these instances, one must seek professional help and begin to work toward emotional healing

The automatic defense against feeling emotional pain is to deny it, but just the opposite is necessary if we are to heal our emotional wounds and derive some meaning from them. This introspective process will also make us stronger and wiser. Facing our emotional pain, that is, understanding it, feeling it, and working through it leads to inner peace, wisdom, and ultimately emotional freedom. Denying it leads to hopelessness, bitterness, and despair or, much worse, a pseudo reality. Once we have worked through our emotional pain, we can let it go.

In essence, we can be dramatically changed forever by a painful or traumatic experience, but we do not have to be forever immobilized by it, and we can choose *how* we will be changed. As noted earlier, in the bitter fight for self-preservation, we may forsake our human dignity - - or we can remain brave, dignified, and unselfish. It is each person's choice.

In conclusion, when we examine all the significant events that we have experienced in our lives, especially those events that caused us the deepest emotional pain, we begin an introspective process that may cause us to suffer and feel deep despair until we discover our own personal answers. As Victor Frankl noted, man's search for meaning may arouse inner tension rather than inner equilibrium but it is precisely this inner tension which is an indispensable prerequisite to emotional health. [19]

Within the sorrow, there is grace. When we come close to those things that break us down, we touch those things that also break us open. And in that breaking open, we uncover our true nature.... This is the point of healing: When we have told the story, we can leave the story behind. What remains is a hidden wholeness, alive, and unbroken. (Wayne Muller, 1996, p. 26)

CHAPTER 4
REGAINING TRUST AND HOPE

"The disease from which modern man suffers is alienation." (Erich Fromm)

The personal life experiences which have caused us to feel deceived, disillusioned, and disappointed, coupled with the publicized corruption, incompetence, and/or apathy that has occurred in our government and our legal court system, as well as in the lives of some religious leaders - - not to mention the sky-rocketing crime, malpractice, and divorce rates - - have caused some of us to be confused about that in which we should believe. Consequently, many of us have lost faith in mankind and the core concepts which represent our human relatedness to each other, that is, love, compassion, equality, justice, etc. Our loss of faith in these core concepts has a devastating effect on us as individuals, as well as on society as a whole. Above all else, it severely damages our basic capacity to trust.

Very early in life, we develop a basic trust or mistrust in others depending on how efficiently our mother or caretaker was at meeting our physical and emotional needs.[1] It is important to note that the development of trust is not dependent upon the quantities of food or demonstrations of love but rather on the *quality* of the maternal relationship.[2] The basic trust or mistrust that we develop early in life is then generalized toward others. We assume the trust we experience within our own home will also be experienced with others in the world outside our home. The same holds true for when we learn to mistrust. In short, the ways in which our parents or caretakers handled, fed, and soothed us as children were all very crucial in shaping our emotional expectations about other people in our social world. [3]

The development of trust is essential to our emotional health and well being because trust is what makes love and intimacy possible. Without trust, there is little or no chance for meaningful and lasting relationships; therefore, the lack of trust often results in solitary despair and isolation, psychologically and/or physically. Consciously or unconsciously, we progressively constrict our social interactions and personal relationships in order to protect ourselves from further emotional pain and disappointment.

Those of us who have been repeatedly hurt by love and life may find ourselves trapped in a self-made prison - - a prison that becomes a refuge which is an escape from the outside world. Yet we realize with time and age, that a life devoid of friendship and love is a life devoid of real meaning and purpose. As Buddha noted, "In separateness lies the world's greatest misery." In the words of the Ecclesiastics, "Woe to him who is alone when he falls and has not another to lift him up." (Ecclesiastes 4:10)

Without trust, true intimacy is impossible; but without hope, everything *seems* impossible. Hope is the indispensable virtue we acquire as a result of learning to trust others.[4] If our emotional needs and desires in childhood are consistently reinforced by trustworthy parents, we will then grow up with hope for an ever expanding array of achievements and accomplishments.[5] In short, as children we learned that it was safe to dare, to dream, to risk, and to gamble - - we trusted that our failures, frustrations, and losses would not be overwhelming because we had hope.[6] On the other hand, if we never learned to trust others in early childhood, then we may have never learned to be hopeful; or if we did learn to trust as children but lost it along the course of our lifetime, then we may have also lost our hopefulness. Without hope, we feel it is not safe to dare, to dream, to risk, and to gamble because we think our failures, frustrations, and losses may be too overwhelming for us to handle. Without hope we are stuck in whatever unhappy circumstances in which we find ourselves.

In essence, we cannot feel hopeful unless we feel secure and we cannot feel secure unless we can trust others - - or at least one other person. In short, trust and hope are tied together and it is the combination of these two inseparable virtues that holds out the promise of personal happiness. The power of hope and its profound impact on the human spirit has been greatly underestimated in many disciplines, including both the sciences of medicine and psychology: "Hope is both the earliest and the most indispensable virtue inherent in the state of being alive...if life is to be sustained hope must remain even when confidence is wounded and trust is impaired."[7]

The loss of hope signifies an emotional surrender and quiet resignation to unhappy life circumstances and/or emotional pain. Without hope, we give up and we only do whatever is necessary to get by. We are just surviving - - but not really living. When we lose hope, we lose the ability to find meaning and purpose in our lives, or worse than this fate, we just accept our lives as being meaningless.

The loss of hope is one of the primary symptoms of depression which is and continues to be a growing problem in today's complex society.[8] Another major symptom of depression is a persistent negative view of the past and present as well as a hopeless view of the future.[9] Individuals who are depressed have difficulty remembering anything positive in their lives as their depression impairs their rational thinking and objectivity.

It has been proposed by a very prominent psychologist that depression is a new plague among Americans.[10] He believed this widespread depression is the result of "epidemic hopelessness" stemming from our culture's advocacy of individualism.[11] Our society strongly advocates independence, "looking out for number one", separation from family, and strong personal identity as opposed to communal cultures which advocate interdependence, extended family closeness, and strong group identity [12] (e.g., as it is in Asia). Although this is an accurate analysis as to how cultural influences can significantly impair our social relationships, it negates the fact that trust and hope are linked together. In other words, "epidemic hopelessness" is more likely the result of our loss of trust in others rather than the isolating characteristics of our culture.

The painful events we experience in life, e.g. betrayal, injustice, indifference, cruelty, etc., cause us to lose trust in others. Just as children generalize their basic trust or mistrust to other people, adults do the very same. Therefore, the loss of trust due to these painful life experiences, as well as other human cruelties, causes us to believe that we are living in an untrustworthy environment. The more painful experiences we have, the more this belief is reinforced.

The word "reinforced" must be emphasized because the process of reinforcement is precisely the way in which we acquire and retain all our beliefs. Reinforcement defined in the dictionary is to strengthen or to encourage.[13] The more something is repeatedly strengthened or encouraged the more difficult it is to extinguish; consequently, it is very difficult to regain trust. Moreover, our rigid adherence to the belief that other people are untrustworthy - - although painful - - seems necessary because it provides us with the consistent knowledge we need to exert some control over our threatening environment. In short, we bring order to the psychological chaos that surrounds us. As noted earlier, "it is not inanimate objects which appear incomprehensible, but people - - it is not nature that appears threatening, but human beings."[14] Similarly, Erich Fromm observed, "As modern society grows more complex, it becomes less human."[15] Therefore, he concluded, we are enveloped in a universe of puzzling phenomena and frightening realities.[16]

When we repeatedly hear on the news about the threat of biological attacks, nuclear warfare, terrorism, suicide bombings, drive-by shootings, world hunger, abandoned babies, parents killing their children, children killing their parents, shooting massacres in schools and other senseless cruelties, there is no way to deny that we are surrounded by a great deal of human irrationality. Human irrationality conflicts with our basic need to make sense of reality and the world in which we live.

Our basic need to understand reality can be traced back to early philosophers. Philosophy first began because of man's curiosity about nature, and then his curiosity about himself and his experiences. In essence, we need to make sense of our reality because we need to feel we have some control over our lives so that some of our negative experiences are not repeated, but how can we make sense of the frightening realities to which we are exposed on a daily basis? How are we supposed to understand a mother strapping her two young children into the back of a car and then pushing the car into the water as she hears them crying for "Mommy"? How do we comprehend a man lining up 12 small children against the wall and then shooting them in the back of their heads? How can we make sense of the terrorists who crashed those airplanes into the Twin Towers on September 11th, 2001, and all the other terrorists who blow themselves up just to kill as many innocent people as they can? What do we feel when we hear about a person who sets a dog on fire just to watch him die?

Human irrationality not only conflicts with our need to make sense of reality but it also conflicts with our need for companionship and love because the understanding we need the most is to make sense of other people.[17] We need to understand and connect with other people, especially in our significant relationships, therefore, we tend to guide our own actions by anticipating the behavior of others.[18] Additionally, we tend to deal with the events that occur in our lives, not as entirely strange and unique occurrences, but as reoccurrences.[19] In other words, we interpret our present experiences based on our past experiences.[20] If we have been repeatedly disappointed by untrustworthy people in our lives, we will automatically assume the same from anyone new - - even if the person has given us no reason to draw that conclusion.

Betrayal is the cruelest blow one human being can give to another. It is a human unkindness that is different from all others, primarily because the emotional pain it causes has been knowingly inflicted by someone whom we trusted, respected, liked, and perhaps loved. However, some individuals rationalize their betrayal by believing their dishonesty and deception is kinder than the truth - - but nothing could be more illogical. No matter how painful, we can intellectually process and make sense of honesty and the truth, but we can never make sense of dishonesty and deception. Therefore, betrayal is the worst type of human unkindness we can experience. Some of us who do experience it never get over it. If we cannot trust our loved ones, our friends, and our families then whom can we trust?

When we have been betrayed, we not only lose our capacity to trust others but we also lose trust in our own perceptions and judgment and this is the most frightening experience of all because in order to emotionally survive in this world, we must be able to trust our perceptions and judgment. Moreover, when we have been betrayed, we feel as though we have been stripped naked in front of the world, not only because of our profound humiliation but also because of our overwhelming feelings of helplessness. Human cruelties not only profoundly change our reality but they also change our self-image.

Many people in today's complex society are living their lives emotionally traumatized by an emotionally devastating experience. When we are not able to recover from an emotionally painful experience or regain our emotional balance, we live in an altered reality for everything that we knew to be true about ourselves and our reality has changed. It is almost like being thrust into a twilight zone where everything on the surface looks the same but everything is profoundly different.

Painful life experiences such as betrayal, injustice, indifference, and cruelty, can devastate our psychological equilibrium and emotional balance because these experiences undermine our sense of security and safety. Because we cannot make sense of the painful events or the people who hurt us, we become uncertain about what to think or how to feel. In short, these human cruelties impair our faculties, both intellectually and emotionally.

Not being able to make sense of our painful experiences, as well as the "craziness" in the world around us, progressively erodes our trust in others. We then resign ourselves to the belief that our fellow man is permanently unknowable and, even more significantly devastating, permanently untrustworthy. With this resignation, we reinstate order and control over our psychologically threatening environment. And since we have a basic need to know and to be known - - which is inseparable from our other basic need, which is to love and to be loved - - we pay the highest conceivable price for this self-imposed order and control. *We cannot love and we cannot be loved.*

Erich Fromm believed, "the deepest need of man is the need to overcome his separateness, to leave the prison of his aloneness".[20] However, the more emotional damage we have suffered, the harder it is to leave the safety and security of our self-made prison, yet, our lives are ultimately meaningless if we cannot trust other people - - if we cannot genuinely care for others, and if we cannot love and be loved. Without the basic capacity to love and be loved, our lives are ultimately meaningless, and every person in this predicament feels this truth deep down in the very core of his or her being. We thus live, and perhaps die, yearning for that which seems out of reach - - for that which we desperately need but for that which appears hopelessly unattainable. Depression is thus inevitable. As Erich Fromm stated, "In the experience of love lies the only answer to being human, lies sanity."[21]

Herein lies the ultimate psychological dilemma and the most perplexing challenge for every person in today's complex society and troubled world. In order to fulfill our two most fundamental needs - - to know and be known and to love and be loved - - we must be able to trust, yet, our trust has been painfully eroded by the many human cruelties that surround us. If we can learn how to trust just *one* other person, e.g. a therapist, a priest, a friend, etc., then we can generalize this experience onto others. We can then take a risk and begin trusting again. This trust will restore our hope because it will renew the possibility that we could care about someone again which also will renew the possibility that we could love again. These renewed possibilities are precisely what help us to leave our prison of aloneness. This truth illustrates how each one of us has the potential to change another person's life for better or for worse, but somehow most of us come to believe that our actions, or inactions, have no significant effect on another when, in fact, one person can significantly change the entire course of another person's life.

For emotional health and happiness, those individuals who have been deeply hurt by life and find themselves in a prison of aloneness, must slowly and ever so carefully crawl out of their self-made prison. The focus of all their mental energy and effort should be directed toward their emotional healing. They should start treating themselves as though they had a serious, life-threatening, medical ailment or some kind of serious paralysis. In fact, you might say, they do have a kind of paralysis. It is just one that has seriously afflicted their hearts and souls.

The bottom line is this: you can remain in the safety and seclusion of your self-made prison or you can make a plan to leave it. This plan may include many things such as psychotherapy, marital therapy, antidepressants, reliance on God or a higher power, building a friendship, fellowship, volunteer work, joining a group - - or any combination thereof. In addition, you need to recognize hurtful people and toxic circumstances so that you can detach from them as much as possible. In short, you must do whatever it may take to help change your life.

We are a society filled with people who have lost faith in mankind and the core concepts which represent our human relatedness to each other - - love, compassion, equality, and justice. The loss of faith in these core concepts is due to repeated experiences with human irrationality which resign us to the belief that our fellow man is permanently unknowable and permanently untrustworthy. Although this personal resignation frequently is unconscious and unspoken, it permeates throughout our entire society and it becomes manifest in our own lives through our fear, depression, anxiety, isolation, mistrust, and apathy. Could it be that our society's alarming degree of depression and loneliness is simply a frightening reflection of our current inability to fulfill our two most fundamental psychological needs - - to know and be known and to love and be loved?

In summary, we must not only acknowledge the many frightening realities that surround us but we must also recognize their impact on our psychological health, and emotional well-being. Many people are overwhelmed by the multitude of demands that are required for both their physical and emotional health and we now see overt manifestations of these overwhelming feelings in people who lose control and resort to desperate acts such as shooting massacres, road rage, murder, etc.

In conclusion, living our lives with some degree of security, contentment, and inner peace can be a monumental challenge for which many of us were not prepared since many of us did not acquire the necessary knowledge for emotional health and personal happiness. Moreover, in today's complex society, we have no way to make sense of the senseless. Therefore, without some psychological understanding about ourselves, others, and the world in which we live, and without just one kind compassionate helping hand, we might spend our entire lifetime running for cover and permanently cut off from the intimate experiences which ultimately make our lives worthwhile and meaningful - - permanently cut off from the prospect of authentic love.

> *I knew that we counted little in comparison with the universe. I knew that we were nothing but to be so immeasurably nothing seems in some way both to overwhelm and at the same time reassure. Those figures, those dimensions beyond the range of human thought, are utterly overpowering. Is there anything whatsoever to which we can cling? Amid that chaos of illusions into which we are cast headlong, there is one thing that stands out as true, and that is - - love (Julian Greene, 1939)*

***

Exercise: When clients were asked, "what would you like to change about the world we live in today?" the following anonymous responses were given.

————

"I would like people to take more responsibility for their lives and their actions. I would like it to be true that the harder you work and the more you strive to be a good person, good things will happen to you. I would like people to be kinder to each other."

————

"First, our world has become far too violent. Violent crimes such as murder and rape are as common in our country as apple pie. I would like people to have more compassion and respect for others. We seem to have lost our sense of shame that my parents talked about after I did something wrong. I believe the media has played a significant role in our loss of shame or guilt. We are bombarded with so much violence through movies, video games, books and even our nightly news that we have become desensitized to the point where violence has become the norm or at least common place. I miss the innocence of my youth."

———

"I would like to stop hearing about tragic events and cruel things that people to do to each other. I would like the people who have wronged me to acknowledge their cruel behavior. I would like to have my sense of innocence back... within myself and within the world I live in. I would like to believe in the goodness of people but I don't anymore."

———

"I think there is way too much violence and cruelty in the world today. Watching the news makes me too sad so I try not to watch it. There is really nothing I can do about all the world problems... it is hard enough for me to deal with my own problems. I have come to believe that human nature is inherently bad because most people are selfish and self-centered. Most people look out for themselves and I think that is why we have the world we live in today. It scares me sometimes because I am still young and I want to make my own way in the world but there is another part of me that wants to recoil and stay at home where I feel more safe."

———

"I would like to change the fact that people are cruel, uncaring and selfish. I would like more people to take responsibility for their actions and their children. I wish people still lived with values and principles instead of their own whims and desires. Most people live for today and do not think about the long-term consequences of their actions. Most people are hurtful and disappointing."

———

"I long for the days when I believed in the goodness of people. Having that belief eroded has also eroded my sense of trust and security. I am more fearful these days and more isolated because my sense of the world has changed. I am hesitant to reach out to others because I have been disappointed so many times in the past. Sometimes I feel trapped as I am unhappy and lonely but cannot seem to change my predicament."

———

"I would like people to be more honest and not use people for their advantage. It seems that people tend to look out for themselves and if they would stop being so self-centered and selfish, we would have a better world. Ironically, I have learned that in order to survive in this world, I have had to become more like the people I am criticizing. You have to look out for yourself and protect yourself otherwise people will walk all over you. For survival, you have to toughen up because life is hard. It is hard to come to this resignation."

On the subject of betrayal, one client wrote:

"I have worked in a small office for 15 years. I worked with one lady for almost as long as I have been there and another lady for 7 years. I felt we had all grown quite close to one another over the years, always discussing our children, husbands, family and even pets. We invited each other to our respective homes for get-togethers and birthdays. We worked together as a team. I considered both of them my best friends and would have put my life in either of their hands without a second thought. One day, the one working for 7 years asked my boss to come out into the main office and when he did, she began to tell him that I was not following office procedure, and that I did not know what I was doing. She was crying and said she could not take the situation in the office any longer. *I was stunned.* I have never felt so betrayed in my entire life. I was made to look like a fool by one friend while my other friend just sat there and did not say a word. Even though the office runs smoothly now with me and my two "best friends", I will never forget their betrayal ….. nor will I ever forgive it." Paula M.

CHAPTER 5
THE PARADOX OF LOVE

"The greatest disease in the West today is not TB or leprosy; it is being unwanted, unloved, and uncared for. We can cure physical disease with medicine, but the only cure for loneliness, despair, and hopelessness is love. There are many in the world who are dying for a piece of bread but there are many more dying for a little love. The poverty in the West is a different kind of poverty ... a poverty of loneliness." (Mother Teresa)

Our most basic emotional need is to love and to be loved. Love is essential to our psychological health and emotional well being, however, love is a paradox. It is something for which we desperately yearn, but for many of us, it appears out of reach.

Love is a powerful human emotion. We can be blessed, enriched, and ultimately fulfilled by love or we can be cursed, drained, and depleted by love. Love can rebuild a life and love can destroy a life. Love can teach us to trust and love can teach us to mistrust. Love can be the ultimate manifestation of beauty, compassion and goodness or, for some individuals, love can be anything but this. For some, love is a human tragedy. This is another truth which makes love a paradox.

For many people, love can be a curious and elusive phenomenon. It can be a mysterious emotion which perplexes the mind and can leave a person in a constant state of yearning for fulfillment. Loving another is one of our most basic innate needs, but, in today's complex society, many of us find ourselves stripped of the capacity to love and to be loved. This is but one more truth which makes love a paradox.

Where do we learn about love? As noted earlier, our first crucial lessons about love occur in our own homes when we were children, and these early lessons become ingrained in our unconscious minds. Our parents, caretakers, and family members, through their own capacities to love and be loved, teach us how lovable we are - - or how unlovable we are - - and this early lesson is most difficult to unlearn. Consequently, those of us who were not loved as children grew up with unfulfilled emotional needs, and we bring these needs to our adult relationships. In other words, because of our childhood conflicts, disappointments, and fears, we bring a personal agenda to our intimate relationships that set forth the conditions that we think will enable us to love and to be loved in return. Therefore, love is rarely unconditional the way it is supposed to be.

The conditions we set forth for our love reflect our attempt at righting old wrongs from the past. Our conditions may be unspoken in the beginning but they always surface with time and, over enough time, these conditions become more important than the love itself. A renowned psychologist noted, however, "that which you love, you are prepared to leave alone".[1]

Where else does a person learn about love? In addition to learning about love from our families, we also learn about love from our society. In our society, romantic love is often portrayed as a blinding and uncontrollable force that makes us feel insensible, lustful, and giddy. This blinding and uncontrollable feeling is often called an infatuation, physical attraction, or a crush, and we often mistake the intensity of this infatuation as proof of our love while, in reality, it may only be proof of our preceding loneliness.[2] Moreover, this kind of love separates the emotion from the person. In other words, whoever this person is that we have fallen in love with is irrelevant because what is most important is the captivating and spellbinding feeling that it gives us.[3]

This socialized idea that romantic love is an instant occurrence begins in childhood with our repeated exposure to fairy tales that unrealistically depict love as an event which magically occurs without opportunity or desire to discover who the loved person really is (e.g., a prince stumbles upon a woman sleeping and they immediately and faithfully commit their love forever). Additionally, television and movies often portray charismatic individuals bumping into each other, consummating a sexual encounter, and then falling deeply in love. Soap operas primarily cast all their characters falling helplessly in love over and over, one after the other. In essence, through the socialization process, many people have acquired a superficial and unrealistic concept of romantic love.

Moreover, because we are socialized to expect this magical romantic love in our lives, we often feel frustrated and incomplete when it is not forthcoming. These expectations also keep us in an indefinite state of waiting which tends to make us feel we should be doing something to find this right person to love -- to find our "soul mate". Technology has capitalized on this phenomenon and now provides many avenues that aid our search and help alleviate our frustrations (e.g. video and internet dating services, personal ad columns, etc.). So, we place an ad in hope that we can find love in the same way we would try to find a car, a lawn mower, or a puppy. Although these techniques may work well for some, they tend to validate the socialized idea that romantic love will come from some sort of magical connection based on a superficial checklist or profile rather than from a feeling of mutual respect and caring which grows deeper over time.

As Erich Fromm explained, our whole society is based on the concept of buying and selling - - on the idea of a mutually favorable exchange.[4] We tend to look at people in a similar manner, and consequently, based on our own assets and limitations, we "fall in love" when we feel we have found the best person available on the market.[5] This "mutually favorable exchange" is one of the reasons why pseudo love is so rampant in our society and why authentic love is such a rare occurrence.

Real love is not a crush, infatuation, sexual attraction, or a mutually favorable exchange. It is none of these things. Real love occurs only when someone penetrates our emotional protective armor, that is, when someone sees beneath our external cover and accepts us as we really are. This is the only way we can feel known; therefore, it is the only way we can feel loved which is why love is the most validating human experience of all. Love enables us to feel real and alive because we are seen and accepted as we really are - - we are known if only for a few seconds.

The experience of being seen and accepted can be life-sustaining because the memory of it becomes crystallized in our minds forever, but the prospect of being seen is precisely why real love is so rare. Being seen as we really are means being exposed and being exposed means being vulnerable. Once we have been deeply hurt by love, we cannot risk being exposed and vulnerable again. Therefore, consciously or unconsciously, we use all kinds of tactics to protect ourselves from the possibility of experiencing more emotional pain.

Some individuals have to emotionally or physically hurt their loved ones in order to make their partner's vulnerability more equal to their own. Some have to repeatedly test their partners' love out of a desperate attempt to determine its authenticity. Others have to distance themselves from the love because they cannot tolerate the intimacy and closeness except in well-timed, protective intervals. Those individuals who cannot tolerate intimacy and everything that a genuine relationship requires, that is, honesty, commitment, and fidelity, use their tactics, consciously or unconsciously, to control the relationship - - and their control ultimately destroys the love. And then there are others who are not aware of having a self that is worthy of love so they are completely oblivious to the prospect of being genuinely loved and/or loving another.

In order to find intimate love we must enter an arena which is fraught with psychological difficulty and emotional danger, and every person who has been deeply hurt by love knows this truth. It is the only arena which requires us to fully surrender ourselves to another, uninhibited and unafraid. It is the only arena which forces us to face another person in a way that reveals our true self. In this arena, we are stripped down to our core essence and we are fully exposed as we really are.

Moreover, because of our instinct for self-preservation, we have a natural fear of losing ourselves to another person.[6] The more personal damage and disappointment we have experienced, the more this need for self-preservation will dominate. However, this is another truth which makes love the greatest paradox of all. Love is an emotion which needs to flow and flourish naturally. If we are to love and be loved, we must be open to it and unafraid. In essence, we cannot be on the defensive and/or ready to retreat, but rather, we must be ready to surrender and be willing to leap into the unknown.[7] However, most of us cannot leap into the unknown because we know with absolute certainty that placing ourselves in a state of "not knowing" means placing ourselves on dangerous ground, psychologically. For these reasons and more, real love is a rare find, especially in today's complex society.

In order to find real love, we must be willing to expose ourselves to another, but if we have experienced a great deal of emotional pain and disappointment this exposure is an impossible task. Consequently, as we grow older, what we miss the most about our youth is our innocence, which is why our first love is so unforgettable and so irretrievable. We were not aware of the danger we were in - - our love was pure emotion and pure passion - - unadulterated by psychological fear and anxiety.

In summary, we have learned through repeated life experiences that in the process of loving another, we place ourselves in a vulnerable position psychologically. Consequently, we must invest much of our mental energy guarding ourselves from the prospect of experiencing any further harm, hurt, and/or humiliation. Not only are we unable to surrender ourselves to another but we also stand on constant emotional guard against the other.

Additionally, we live in a promiscuous and "throw away society", that is, a society which easily discards people, animals, and things, so we realize that we too could be easily discarded and replaced by another. This fear further incapacitates our ability to fully trust and love another however, our yearning for love and physical contact still presses for fulfillment. So in a desperate attempt to satisfy this yearning, some individuals turn to pseudo love and pseudo passion (i.e. lust, sexual promiscuity, and fleeting infatuations), but pseudo love and pseudo passion are merely bad substitutes for real love and real passion and like any bad substitute it rarely, if ever, suppresses the hunger for the real thing. Consequently, these individuals begin to feel like they are living their lives in a revolving door as people are continuously coming and going in and out of their lives - - and sometimes in and out of their beds. These temporary relationships can be very unsettling because what these individuals really hunger for the most is authentic love - - love they can count on forever.

Sexual promiscuity signifies a quiet resignation to the superficial and to the transient. It also speaks to a lack of regard and respect for ourselves, as well as for others. But more than this, sexual promiscuity is a consequence of man's current chronic condition in today's complex society - - a consequence of his inability to find and sustain authentic love. As Viktor Frankl noted, sexual desire tends to become rampant whenever emptiness and personal despair is prevalent.[8]

> *Because sexual desire is in the minds of most people coupled with the idea of love, they are easily misled to conclude that they love each other when they want each other physically.... Sexual attraction creates, for a moment, the illusion of union, yet without love this "union" leaves strangers as far apart as they ever were before - sometimes it makes them ashamed of each other, or even makes them hate each other, because when the illusion has gone they feel their estrangement even more markedly than before.... The sexual act without love never bridges the gap between two human beings, except momentarily. (Erich Fromm, 1956, pp.45-46, 10)*

Once we become comfortable with the prospect of entering into sexual relationships with strangers, there are no more natural inhibitions or moral guidelines upon which to direct our social behavior. Once these barriers have been broken, every person has the potential of being our sexual partner which means fidelity, honesty, and commitment become abstract ideals. In short, when we are not accustomed to behaving with sexual restraint, we will find it increasingly more difficult to do so, and we come to believe that being monogamous is a great sacrifice. This phenomenon may be one of the major reasons for our society's alarming rate of divorce.

As another prominent psychologist noted, an unavoidable source of disappointment and mistrust comes from the very intensity of love which stirs up all our secret expectations and longings for happiness but the very nature of these expectations and longings makes them impossible for anyone to fulfill.[9] We must come to terms with this fact, and as we do so, we must distinguish between that which only we can do to fulfill ourselves and that which can be done by another. Similarly, Erich Fromm believed there is hardly any other activity or commitment besides love, which begins with such tremendous hope and expectation yet fails so regularly.[10] ·

Our fear of love will always be mixed with the fear of what we might do to the other person or what the other person might do to us.[11] As we try to achieve true intimacy with another, we often vacillate between our need for closeness and our need for separation.[12] In other words, on the one hand we have a fear of being engulfed or smothered by another and, on the other hand we have a fear of being rejected or abandoned.[13] These two conflicting fears are often unconscious, but they are the powerful forces which often disturb, disrupt, and destroy intimate relationships. In many ways then, true intimacy can only be obtained by a mutually achieved balance between individuality and togetherness. However, in order for this balance to be achieved there must be a basic trust and commitment, otherwise these fears will permeate the relationship and ultimately destroy it.

In conclusion, most of us learn very little, if anything at

all, about love and intimacy. It is a subject that everyone should study, but where is it taught except in unrealistic childhood fairy tales, television soap operas, and big screen Hollywood movies.

People think that to love is simple, but to find the right person to love – or to be loved by - is difficult.... The first step to take is to become aware that love is an art.... If we want to learn how to love we must proceed in the same way we have to proceed if we want to learn any other art ... aside from learning the theory and practice, there is a third factor necessary to becoming a master in any art – there must be nothing else in the world more important than the art.... And, maybe here lies the answer to the question of why people in our culture try so rarely to learn this art, in spite of their obvious failures: in spite of their deep-seated cravings for love, almost everything is considered to be more important than love: success, prestige, money, power – almost all of our energy is used for the learning of how to achieve these aims, and almost none to learn the art of loving.... Could it be that... love, which only profits the soul, but is profitless in the modern sense, is a luxury we have no right to spend much energy on? (Erich Fromm 1956, p.2, 4-5)

***

The following are genuine responses to the question, "What have your intimate relationships taught you about love?" The names are fictitious.

———

"The one experience that profoundly undermined my ability to trust other people was my divorce. It was painful, unexpected, and left my heading spinning for years. This experience taught me that one person can never have control over another. One cannot trust another to do or be anything that they do not have the heart to be or do." Bob J.

———

"The one thing I do not understand about women is that their emotions generally drive their actions rather than logic or reason. One lesson I learned from my experiences is that men think and women feel." Carl B.

———

"My experiences with men in general, starting with my father, taught me not to trust the opposite sex. I do not understand how closed off men are from their emotions. Not everything can be dealt with using logic or reason… especially matters of the heart." Mary T.

———

"Love has taught me that people are really hard to know. You give your heart to someone and bare your soul and what you get in return is just not worth the emotional pain that it causes. My past failed relationships have left me feeling very lonely and afraid to date again. I am mistrustful and just not able to risk being that hurt and vulnerable again. Age has made me stronger in many ways but not with matters of the heart. It just seems easier to accept being alone versus going through all that trouble and disappointment." Greg S.

———

"My divorce changed me for the worse because it was a bitter battle that cost me a lot of money. I was very good to this person who treated me so rotten. It made me very cautious and suspicious of other women. My wife had a hidden meanness that was not obvious at the start. I now believe most women are looking for men who can take care of them therefore they are not interested in men who do not have money. Women are shallow. When I had money, I had no problem getting women and when I was broke women were not interested. But I also know that men are shallow too. They are only interested in women who are pretty, ironically enough, that is why I married my wife." Dan R.

"For the past year, I have been trying to stop feeling so much anger toward my husband. When he left me last year, I felt so much pain, rejection, and anger because he hurt me so much. After having two husbands walk out on me, I have learned that the only person in the world I can count on is me." Debbie W.

"I loved my husband before we even had an intimate relationship. Intimacy, in my estimation, does not necessarily mean love. Love means trusting, caring, and sharing - - and most importantly communication." Sue S.

"A relationship that starts with excitement is doomed from the start. Excitement fades and gives way to hopes that will never be fulfilled. A misunderstanding is always at hand because the excitement in the beginning that was there is expected to go on - - and it does not. A solid relationship with a good honest man is the way to go. But if it is an uncertain time in our life (like a mid-life crisis), we tend to act upon this "excitement" that enters our life and forego the "rock solid" relationship we already have because it has become boring. Yet, romance is what we make it! You can stir up a dull relationship with a little imagination - - there is really no need to go looking for it elsewhere." Pam D.

———

"I used to believe in love when I was young. Now that I have reached middle age, I am very jaded and cynical about love. Real love is rare, and looking for it is a painful journey because there is so much deception and dishonesty. Each broken relationship leaves you more guarded and less able to reach out to another person, even when that person gives you every indication that this time will be different. I am afraid that I have reached the point where I would not recognize real love if it hit me between the eyes. But still, I keep looking. Tom D.

CHAPTER 6
RECLAIMING YOUR SOUL

"This life is a test. It is only a test. Had it been an actual life, you would have received further instructions on where to go and what to do." (Author Unknown)

No matter how hard we may try to understand this life, or how much progress we make in science and technology, many of our questions confound the human mind because they are too incomprehensible to grasp, e.g., creation, gestation, astronomy, and death. Nevertheless, we all know our inevitable fate. We enter into this world alone and through death we leave this world alone. We know this basic truth no matter what happens to us in between, no matter if we are surrounded by love, no matter if we are immersed in purposeful activity, and no matter how many of our existential questions are answered or remain unanswered.

In addition to living with existential uncertainty, we must also live with the more pervasive uncertainty of today's world, that is, the ominous threats of terrorism, biological attacks, nuclear war, etc. Add to this the pain and heartaches of our own personal trials and tribulations and it is easy to see why some of us are struggling to emotionally survive. It is easy to see why some of us need an escape from reality or some form of protective armor, and this need for emotional protection is more compelling today than ever before.

Some individuals emotionally survive by emotionally shutting down. They have repressed so much emotional pain for so long they can no longer feel anything. They no longer feel sadness, anger, or bitterness toward others or toward anything. They just feel nothing and this nothingness, or this monotone existence, is a private hell all its own. Usually when an individual's psyche resorts to this kind of emotional numbing, it is because he or she was once overwhelmed with too much emotional pain or psychological trauma.

No matter how different we are in dealing with our personal trials and tribulations, we all share a strong common bond. We have a basic need to feel that we somehow matter - - we need to feel connected to something greater than ourselves - - and we question at one time or another whether there really is something beyond this life. Those individuals who have a deep faith in God believe there is life after death and that Heaven is their ultimate destination. Others either disbelieve it or stay too busy to think about it. They have neither the time nor the inclination to do any soul searching or to ponder any existential questions.

The term soul, despite its lack of definition, can be conceived of as a crucial part of an individual's real self or core essence. Whether the terms real self and soul are synonymous or interchangeable could be regarded as a question of semantics and dependent upon one's personal beliefs. For those individuals who do not believe in God, the term "real self" would more accurately describe their core essence. Others who do believe in God would choose the word "soul".

No matter how we conceptualize it, the real self or the soul is that part of our being that needs to feel meaningful and purposeful. Viktor Frankl explained it like this:

What man actually needs is not a tensionless state but rather the striving and struggling for a worthwhile goal, a freely chosen task. What he needs is not the discharge of tension at any cost but the call of a potential meaning waiting to be fulfilled by him. (Viktor Frankl, 1959, p.127)

Many individuals, especially in today's fast-paced society, satisfy their need for meaning by staying constantly busy. Their meaning and purpose in life is grounded in whatever activity or work they have chosen to do, however, when that activity stops because of retirement, leave of absence, illness, etc. many of these individuals will feel lost or displaced. If they do not find some other source of meaning or purpose for their lives, depression is inevitable.

If we feel our lives have meaning and purpose, then we can more easily deal with whatever frightening predicaments that may confront us. One psychologist believed that finding meaning in one's life requires, "an attachment to something larger than the lonely self...the self is a very poor site for finding meaning".[1]

There is nothing in the world, I would venture to say, that would so effectively help one to survive even the worst conditions as the knowledge that there is meaning to one's life. There is much wisdom in the words of Nietzsche: "He who has a why to live for can bear almost any how." (Viktor Frankl, 1959, p.126)

Finding the "why to live for" is related to our values, and our values are largely determined by the way we were socialized by our families and our society. Our personal values are reflective of how well we know and understand ourselves, and they reveal that which we consider most important in our lives. In short, our values are the product of the thinking we have done - - or the thinking we have failed to do.[2]

> *Values can be an expression of psychological maturity or of arrested development. They can grow out of self-confidence and benevolence or out of self-doubt and fear. They can be motivated by the desire to achieve happiness or by the desire to minimize pain. They can be born out of the desire to use one's mind or the desire to escape it. They can be acquired independently and by deliberation or they can be uncritically absorbed from other men... They can be consistent or they can be contradictory. They can further a man's life or they can endanger it. (Nathaniel Branden, 1969, 66-67)*

In addition to our values, the meaning we attach to our lives is also the product of the thinking we have done or failed to do because, unlike other animals, we ponder existential questions.

> *An animal's basic values and goals are biologically "programmed" by nature. An animal does not face such questions as: What kind of entity should I seek to become? For what purpose should I live? What should I make of my life? Man does and men answer these questions in vastly different ways, depending on the quantity and quality of their thinking. (Nathaniel Branden,, 1969, p.67)*

People who feel a deep belief in God find all the meaning and purpose they need. When they turn to God, all their burdens are lifted as stress, despair, and insecurity disappear.[3] They do not have to define their self-worth solely by their success, status, or social approval.[4] To find inner security and self-acceptance they need not do or be anything.[5] Their self-worth comes from believing that God loves them and accepts them unconditionally.[6]

In short, those individuals who turn toward a creator, God, or a higher power find the answers and the comfort they seek. Others, too pragmatic in their thinking to ever accept the concept of God are not so fortunate. They must find meaning for their lives elsewhere or painfully accept themselves, in the big picture, as meaningless. However, some non-believers cannot dismiss God so easily because they have difficulty accepting their lives as meaningless and without purpose. They sometimes become frightened by the general emptiness they feel. Although some form of spirituality would provide them with the answers and comfort they need, they have too many intellectual and/or emotional barriers obstructing their spiritual growth.

Sometimes, the pragmatic non-believer chooses not to believe because of all the human irrationality and natural disasters that exist in the world. God's silence is perplexing. If God does really exist, where is He; and if He is all loving and all powerful, why does He allow so many bad things to happen? If He is so loving and powerful, why doesn't He protect us?

Some individuals have been so hurt by life they feel anger, cynicism, and/or bitterness toward God. They cannot understand how a loving God could let them suffer, but, according to religious writings, suffering is not only the impetus for spiritual exploration and growth but it is also a necessary prerequisite for steadfast faith, "Where there is no struggle, there is no strength." Religious writings repeatedly state that suffering is an integral part of being human and we cannot escape it. Ironically, the ultimate suffering for some individuals is feeling estranged from God, especially if the estrangement is based on the conclusion that He has abandoned them, that He does not exist or, worst of all, that He is punishing them.

> *The idea that God gives people what they deserve, that our misdeeds cause our misfortune, is a neat and attractive solution to the problem of evil at several levels, but it has a number of serious limitations. As we have seen, it teaches people to blame themselves. It creates guilt where this is no basis for guilt. It makes people hate God, even as it makes them hate themselves. And most disturbing of all, it does not even fit the facts. (Rabbi Kushner, 1981, p.10)*

For those individuals who are confirmed atheists, God has no place or purpose in their lives and they have resigned themselves to a finite existence. They believe there is nothing beyond this life - - there is no soul and there is no life after death. Generally, these individuals tend to be intellectual, logical, and very pragmatic. They relate the concept of God to a fairy tale and they tend to regard people who believe in God as irrational and weak. They question how anyone with any logic could possibly believe there is a God when He never makes His presence known except of course to the blind faith of irrational and weak believers.

If there is a God, where is He and what does He look like? Is He an old man with a long beard sitting on a throne way up in the sky? It is doubtful that even the strongest believers see God this way. In fact, most believers do not see God in any way - - they *feel* Him. They *know* He exists because they feel it. So if nothing else, the atheists and agnostics must at least acknowledge that a belief in God is not a decision that comes from illogical thinking but is instead a feeling that comes from within. Therefore, the atheist who has concluded that God does not exist must allow for the possibility that his conclusion is not only based on his logical thought processes but may also be based on an emotional void.

Why is it that atheists and agnostics do not feel God as the believers do? Is it because their strong sense of logic obstructs any feeling for God they might otherwise have? Or perhaps their feelings for God have been over-powered by other feelings - - feelings that have filled their hearts with so much pain and unhappiness there is no room for anything else, especially not for the concept of an all-powerful God who is supposed to love them but chose to let them suffer.

Nevertheless, the atheist believes he is logical, but his thinking actually defies logic. To believe there is no God is to believe there is no creator, that life is an accident, that sex, being an unfailing guarantee of procreation is not by intentional design but just an accidental and extraordinary coincidence - - that the innate instinct in every species on earth to survive at any cost, together with the innate instinct of a mother to protect her young at any cost, both of which clearly preserve and perpetuate life, are also not by intentional design but are just coincidental to the concept that life is an accident. If the atheist wants to be logical, he needs to think about these "accidental coincidences" which clearly serve the deliberate purpose of procreating and perpetuating life, as it may give him reason to re-examine his concept of the God in whom he does not believe.

In summary, there are many individuals who believe very deeply in God, and from that belief they derive a profound sense of meaning, inner peace and emotional well being. On the other hand, there are many individuals who feel very certain that God does not exist nor do they need to believe He exists to derive any sense of meaning, inner peace and emotional well being.

Then there is a third category of individuals who fall somewhere in between. They have the non-believers' logic with the believers' heart-felt needs. They are plagued by what Viktor Frankl described as an "existential vacuum" which is an inner emptiness that causes them to vacillate between boredom and distress.[7] They constantly strive to understand their temporary existence but nothing seems to really satisfy them. In the words of C.S. Lewis, "I find within myself a desire which no earthly experience can satisfy." Saint Augustine theorized, "The soul cannot find its peace among the pleasures of flesh or sensation." (Yet, in today's society, the pleasures of flesh and sensation are the places where many individuals often turn for meaning and self-fulfillment).

Nothing can persuade the atheist to believe just as nothing can persuade the believer not to believe, but for those individuals who feel a need to believe in something greater than themselves and who are filled with a desire which no earthly experience can satisfy, some form of spirituality may provide them with the answers and comfort they seek.

Rabbi Kushner noted that religious faith satisfies the most fundamental need of man, which is the need to know that he somehow matters, that his life means something, that he "counts as something more than just a momentary blip in the universe."[8] Erich Fromm believed we need "an object of devotion, a goal or God to which we can attach meaning, to whom we can attribute the meaning of life." [9] Carl Jung asserted that our need for God is directly related to our need for self-fulfillment because without God to aspire to we are forever condemned to the incompleteness of our own existence."[10] "To take the leap into active faith is to bet one's life on a world view that makes sense of the universe, that gives meaning to life, that offers hope in the face of adversity and death, that provides vision and courage for living in the present."[11]

A person who has suffered a great deal of emotional pain and/or personal loss may find solace in the healing power of some form of spiritual practice and this healing power is far beyond man's understanding. Viktor Frankl explained it like this:

Man can preserve a vestige of spiritual freedom, of independence of mind, even in such terrible conditions of psychic and physical stress....Fundamentally, therefore, any man can decide what shall become of him - mentally and spiritually... It is this spiritual freedom - - which cannot be taken away - - that makes life meaningful and purposeful. (Victor Frankl, 1959, p86-87)

When we have experienced too much emotional pain, we tend to lose sight of the goodness that exists in many people, and we would be more open and receptive to this goodness if we were healed from our many hurts and disappointments.

There is a light in this world, a healing spirit more powerful than any darkness we may encounter. We sometimes lose sight of this force when there is suffering, too much pain. Then suddenly, the spirit will emerge through the lives of ordinary people who hear a call and answer in extraordinary ways. (Mother Teresa, 1996, p.235)

It is interesting to note that Alcoholics Anonymous (A.A.) and Narcotics Anonymous (N.A.) are the most successful treatment programs to date for addictions, and they both follow a twelve step recovery program which, above all, brings spirituality into the forefront of its members' lives. A member begins to feel he is no longer alone on his life's journey, but he is instead, accompanied by a constant source of strength upon which he can lean and always trust. This source of strength often helps these members to deal more effectively with the very difficulties that fuel or exacerbate their addictions.

A meaningful belief in God or a higher power requires us to have a certain degree of mature self-understanding. We should make an honest self-appraisal of our strengths and weaknesses, as well as acknowledge our faults, failures, and human frailty. Herein lies a unique opportunity for us to learn more about ourselves psychologically. Consciously, but more often times unconsciously, we may have transferred onto God that which we have experienced with our parents, as well as other important authority figures. For example, if we experienced abandonment, betrayal, indifference, or punitiveness by our parents or other important authority figures, we will then be likely to expect the same from God. Since God is the ultimate blank screen, that is, the ultimate unknown and faceless entity, He is the most likely recipient for all our displaced feelings of resentment, bitterness, and anger.

When an individual is not aware of this psychological phenomenon, he often turns away from God or religion with many unresolved emotions, but these unresolved emotions continue to become manifest in his other personal relationships. If a person turns his back on God out of anger, pride, bitterness, or disappointment then he will most likely resolve his personal relationships the same way, that is, he will simply walk away, detach, cut himself off, or find alternative outlets or substitutes.

Similarly, Mother Teresa noted that it is important for a person to gain self-knowledge because if he can know himself and believe in himself, then it means he can also know and believe in God.[12] Sister Kateri stated, "Knowledge of yourself produces humility and knowledge of God produces love."[13] Both kinds of knowledge strengthen a person's faith in something larger than himself and help him to make an honest appraisal about that which is fostering or impeding his spiritual development. Consequently, self-knowledge and humility are important aspects of a relationship with God or a higher power because both help an individual to surrender his will to that of another.

Just as the act of surrendering is necessary for a close intimate relationship with another person, it is also necessary in a spiritual relationship. In short, a person must be able to acknowledge his human frailty and his basic helplessness so that he can learn to lean on another source of strength. For many individuals this step is not an easy one to take, but if they can get past their pragmatism and replace some of their logic with some degree of faith, then their exhaustive search can be turned into a meaningful and purposeful life journey.

Nevertheless, a disbelief in God does not necessarily imply a disbelief in God-like creeds. One does not have to believe in God to follow God's creeds and to be a good person. In fact, some atheists and agnostics have far more goodness in their characters than some self-professed believers.

One of the most important religious creeds centers on forgiveness. When we forgive those who have wronged us, we can slowly begin to reclaim our souls. "When we forgive someone we change the course of a meandering river that could, if we let it, carry us on an aimless, endless current of remembered hurt and frustrated rage."[14]

Forgiving does not erase the bitter past. A healed memory is not a deleted memory. Instead, forgiving what we cannot forget

creates a new way to remember. We can change the memory of
our past into a hope for our future.... As we begin to forgive, we
get the grit to aim the blame straight in the eyes of our culprit....
Nobody can ever do anything more worthy of self-respect than
to break the grip of a painful past that he or she never deserved
and walk dangerously with hope into the possibility of tomorrow.
(Lewis Smedes,1996, pp.171, 174)

Many individuals seek counseling to help them break the grip of a painful past. An essential goal of counseling is to help a person heal from his emotional wounds but no matter how competent a psychologist may be, for some individuals it is only a belief in God or a higher power that will ultimately heal them. Sometimes the physical act of praying to God, or whoever they think may be listening, is the first step toward healing and leaning on something greater than themselves. Healing is an emotional journey - - not just an intellectual one. Wayne Muller, a well-known theologian, explained that an essential part of spiritual development and growth is "cutting away what must be cut, and letting remain what must remain."[15] Knowing what to cut or get rid of requires wisdom, but being clear and strong enough to make the cut when it is time for things to go, requires courage.[16]

In conclusion, when a person turns to God or a higher power, he can finally remove himself from the world of "things" - - or his man-made world which solely defines him as a certain "thing" in the social structure. Insomuch as God is unrecognizable and indefinable, and inasmuch as man is made in the likeness of God, man is indefinable - - which means he is not and can never be considered a thing in the social structure.[17] Therefore, a person no longer has to define his self-worth solely by his success, status, or social approval because to find self-acceptance he need not do anything or be anything; he simply needs to realize that he is loved and accepted unconditionally by God.[18]

Finally, and on a lighter note, the following story humorously reflects how difficult it can be to have steadfast faith, even in times of great need:

A man fell off a cliff and managed to grab hold of a small tree on the rim. As he hung there, he looked up and screamed, "Is anyone up there to help me?"

There was silence. So he yelled again,
"Please, is there anyone up there?"
Soon a voice thundered from the sky.
"I am here."
"Who are you?" the man asked.
"I am your Lord, the great I Am, your God."
"Is that really you Lord?" the man yelled.
"Yes."
"Save me, Lord" the man cried.
"I will save you," God said. "Just let go."
The man thought for a moment. Then he replied,
"Is anyone else up there?"
(Author Unknown)

Exercise 6: What are your feelings toward God?

"The most painful experience I have ever had was losing my son. He was murdered at the age of 22. I do not know if my husband and I could have gone on with our lives if we had not turned to God. We had not been to church for more than eight years but the day after we buried him that is precisely where we went… where we had to go. We were so desperate to feel close to our son again and we knew that there was no other place on the earth that he could be so He had to be with God and so we had to be with God too. We needed to believe that he was with God and that God would take care of him. And if he was with God, we knew we would see him again. We were so plagued with sadness, anger, and guilt ….. we both knew that nothing could restore our peace but God." Audrey B.

———

"I believe in God but I do not believe he interferes with free will which is why we often choose poorly. I believe we choose our general path in life and must take responsibility for our decisions. I am turned off by organized religion but I believe in having a spiritual relationship with God." Jennifer L.

———

"I believe God is my father who protects me and my family. He is my partner in life. I believe He lives inside of me and He answers my prayers. I do not know how people can live without God. I am often alone but I am never lonely. I always feel God is with me." Greg

———

"I am not sure there is a God. My personal experiences make me doubt that a God would allow people to suffer the way so many do. I have also experienced a good deal of hypocrisy. I have seen "Christians" do horrible things to other people e.g. steal money, lie, cheat, etc. I guess I ultimately cut myself off from God because He let me go through so much difficulty in my life. I was raised Catholic but have not been in a church for years. I guess I feel God has failed me. I did everything right but He was not there for me. I guess I am angry and bitter over that fact." John J.

CHAPTER 7
PSYCHOLOGY AND ITS PURPOSE

"The fact is that modern man exhibits an amazing lack of realism for all that matters ... for the meaning of life and death, for happiness and suffering, for feeling and serious thought".(Erich Fromm)

The field of psychology and its purpose seems to be a mystery to many people. Some individuals have little idea as to what psychologists do while others sometimes scoff, impugn, or ridicule what they imagine psychologists do. Psychology defined is the science of the mind, emotions, and behavior. It applies to every person and it is a part of every person's being, yet many people seem to know little about this subject. Moreover, and more importantly, they know little about their own personal psychology - - about why they feel and behave as they do.

There are many theories which describe man's basic nature, as well as the important events which impact and shape his personality. One theory describes man as hopelessly ruled by primitive impulses and drives while another describes man as being self-determined and therefore having control of his own destiny. Abraham Maslow defined the truly healthy personality as "one that possesses sufficient personal fortitude and creativity to be innocent" believing innocence refers to the person's capacity to live without pretense - - to be genuinely bereft of guilt in thought, word, and deed.[1] Carl Rogers emphasized a person's inherent capacity to direct his own life, and he believed that the primary essential ingredient of the well-lived life is simply the freedom to be.[2] Carl Jung theorized the purpose of an individual's life is attained when that person is fully integrated and completely in harmony with his real self.[3]

Alfred Adler, another prominent theorist, believed man has one fundamental purpose and that is to grow, to become whole, and to seek happiness by becoming what he is supposed to be.[4] Erik Erikson stated for life to be meaningful and worthwhile, the individual must feel he has the power within himself to shape his own destiny - - the psychologically healthy individual "sees that the person he was, the person he is, and the person he is becoming are smooth continuations of the person he must be in face of the realities that are his."[5]

Because the field of psychology focuses on our thoughts, feelings and behaviors - - that is, our internal reality - - its importance is often overshadowed by society's primary focus on our appearance, success, and status - - that is, our external reality. Consequently, we are socialized to believe that self-esteem is achieved through the external. As noted earlier, in this society income, occupation, and status are all of paramount importance with regard to how well we feel we are doing in life, and how well we think we fit in and belong.

> *Man experiences himself as a thing to be successfully employed on the market. He does not experience himself as an active agent, as the bearer of human powers. He is alienated from these powers. His aim is to sell himself successfully on the market. His sense of self does not stem from his activity as a loving and thinking individual, but from his socio-economic role. If things could speak, a typewriter would answer the question, "Who are you?"*

by saying, "I am a typewriter," and an automobile by saying, "I am an automobile," or more specifically by saying, "I am a Ford," or "a Buick," or "a Cadillac." If you ask a man "Who are you?", he answers, "I am a manufacturer," I am a clerk", or "I am a doctor" - or "I am a married man," "I am the father of two kids," and his answer has pretty much the same meaning as that of the speaking thing would have. That is the way he experiences himself, not as a man with love, fear, convictions, doubts, but as that abstraction, alienated from his real nature, which fulfills a certain function in the social system. His sense of value depends on his success: on whether he can sell himself favorably, whether he can make more of himself than he started out with… His body, his mind, and his soul are his capital, and his task in life is to invest it favorably, to make a profit for himself. (Erich Fromm, 1955, pp.141-142)

Because our socio-economic status is of utmost importance to our sense of worth and self-esteem, there is a powerful belief in our society that routine "functioning" signifies success and normalcy. This socialized belief explains why we panic and sometimes emotionally crumble when formal structure which ensures our routine functioning is removed from our lives, e.g., unemployment, retirement, leave of absence, etc. It also explains why many of us will neither slow down nor temporally stop when we are psychologically hurting. Instead, we tend to use all kinds of quick fixes and escapes to mask our emotional pain, so much so that some of us organize our whole life in such a way that it becomes one big total distraction itself. In other words, if we cannot figure out our place and purpose in life, and if we cannot make sense of our unhappiness, then the second best solution is to stay so busy that we won't have the time to try or to be bothered by it.

Man becomes a "nine to fiver", he is part of the labor force, or the bureaucratic force of clerks and managers... there is little difference between those high up on the ladder and those on the bottom. They all perform tasks prescribed by the whole structure of the organization, at a prescribed speed, and in a prescribed manner. Even the feelings are prescribed: cheerfulness, tolerance, reliability, ambition, and an ability to get along with everybody without friction. Fun is routinized in similar, although not quite as drastic ways. Books are selected by the book club, movies by the film and theater owners... the rest is also uniform: the Sunday ride in the car, the television sessions, the card games, the social parties. From birth to death, from Monday to Monday, from morning to evening - all activities are routine and prefabricated. How should a man caught in this net of routine not forget that he is a man, a unique individual, one who is given this only one chance of living, with hopes and disappointments, with sorrow and fear, with the longing of love...?(Erich Fromm, 1956, p. 14)

In the words of singer/ songwriter John Lennon: "Life is what happens to you while you are making other plans." Similarly, Pascal observed, "So we never live, but we hope to live - - and we are always preparing to be happy, it is inevitable that we should never be so."

Erich Fromm believed the major difficulty with our society is that the requirements it purports to be normal often conflict with our basic needs for personal growth and happiness.[6] In other words, the capitalistic nature of our society forces isolating competition among individuals whose human nature desperately requires nurturance, cooperation, and mutual caring.[7] Yet, our current definition of normalcy is solely based on the idea that so long as a person does not violate the laws and social norms of his particular society, then he is sane.[8]

This definition of normalcy assumes that society's norms and laws are correct.[9] However, as Erich Fromm believed, normalcy should not be defined in terms of how well an individual adjusts to his society but, on the contrary, it must be defined in terms of how well a society adjusts to meet the basic needs of man.[10] In other words, as Freud originally noted, it may be the society that is abnormal and maladjusted - - not the individual.[11]

> *A healthy society furthers man's capacity to love his fellow man, to work creatively, to develop his reason and objectivity, to have a sense of self which is based on the experience of his own productive powers. An unhealthy society is one which creates mutual hostility, distrust, which transforms man into an instrument of use and exploitation for others, which deprives him of a sense of self, except insomuch as he submits to others or becomes an automaton (robot)... The statement that man can live under almost any condition is only half true; it must be supplemented with another statement, that if he lives under conditions which are contrary to his nature and to the basic requirements for human growth and sanity, he cannot help reacting; he must either deteriorate.... or bring about conditions which are more in accordance with his needs. (Erich Fromm,1955, pp. 72-73, 19)*

In our society there is a great imbalance between the knowledge we acquire for physical survival versus the knowledge we acquire for emotional survival. We learn how to physically navigate throughout our lifetimes but psychologically, we are in the dark; yet paradoxically, it is our psychological knowledge, that is, the general understanding of ourselves and others which ultimately determines the quality of our lives.

Ideally, as children, we should have acquired a basic understanding of ourselves and others within our own family; however, far too many home environments fail to provide this kind of psychological knowledge. As a result, some of us grew up dreadfully unprepared to emotionally cope with life's trials and tribulations, as well as the dysfunctional people we meet in our complex society and troubled world.

As adults, we can acquire the psychological knowledge we need in psychotherapy, but this method is retroactive, that is, after the fact. Is it not far better to grow up in a society that provides an arena that fosters our healthy emotional development in childhood as opposed to adulthood, or never at all? If so many parents are unable to provide a home environment where children can learn about themselves, others, and the social world in which they live, then school provides the only other opportunity where children can learn these essential lessons. In other words, we can compensate for this deficit in the only other arena that monopolizes the majority of a child's time, that is, in our public school system.

Vocational Counseling in the school is not enough. Before we can know what we can become, we must first know who we are. Instead, many of us went to school holding in and repressing that which pained and perplexed us most, thereby becoming obscured in another dysfunctional social setting. Not only were we discouraged from expressing our feelings and thoughts in the classroom, but it was often prohibited. Many of us went through school in the same mechanistic way that factories put cars through assembly lines, and many of our children today are going through school in the same way.

An important part of maturation and growth is psychological yet our public educational system minimizes this crucial aspect of learning. Our public school curriculum, as it is presently taught and organized, places a higher value on objective measures of intelligence, e.g. grades, IQ scores, etc. Understanding the correct order of the alphabet is more important than understanding the correct way to interact with others. Learning how to spell courtesy is more important than learning how to show it. Calculating the right answer to a math problem is more important than contemplating behavioral conduct and moral reasoning. In short, our educational system is seriously deficient in the most essential teachings necessary for emotional health. As a result, far too many children in school today have no interest in the pursuit of knowledge because it has little or no practical value in their current reality. The lessons simply pass through them. They do not embrace or retain any knowledge because the lessons do not contain any material or information that has personal relevance in their lives.

There is no reason why the subjects of psychology and sociology cannot be reduced to an elementary level of understanding, beginning in the first grade and progressing upward. Many of us needed this psychological intervention when we were children, and the children today need it even more. In short, children need to learn about social interactions with other people in a way that is educationally structured as opposed to the usual and haphazard way that can be confusing and emotionally damaging.

> *The encounter with human irrationality, in childhood, is one of the earliest psychological traumas in the lives of many people, and one of the earliest occasions of repression. At a time when a young mind is struggling to acquire a firm grasp of reality, it is often confronted - through the actions of parents and other adults - with what appears to be an incomprehensible universe. It is not inanimate objects which appear incomprehensible, but people. It is not nature that appears threatening, but human beings. And, more often than not, the problem is submerged by him, repressed,*

ignored, never dealt with, never understood, never conquered
(Nathaniel Branden,1969, p. 90)

Children need to learn about the many different feelings that people may have and the many different ways that people express those feelings in their interactions with each other. In very careful and selective ways, children could be told stories and shown film clips to give them some understanding of the various emotional problems that other children and adults may have. Why is that lady crying? Why is that man angry? Why is that boy so sad? These are the kinds of questions and issues that are addressed by psychologists in counseling sessions with troubled children. Well-trained teachers could be asking these same questions in classrooms that are usually more than half filled with troubled children.

Teenagers staking territorial claims are shooting each other on city streets, hitting and sometimes killing innocent people who happen to be in the area. Students are carrying deadly weapons into the classroom. Police are stationed on the school grounds for security purposes. Our juvenile court system is overburdened with cases that are prosecuting children as young as eight years old, sometimes for murder. The statistics are staggering. Despite the enormous proliferation of drug abuse, juvenile crime, and sexual promiscuity which clearly signal a serious deficiency in so many home environments, we continue to ignore the frightful reality of our social conditions and cling to an ideal tradition that morality and good behavior should be taught in the home - - an ideal tradition that progressively fails with each passing generation.

Those teenagers shooting each other on the streets were sitting in classrooms just a few short years before. When they entered elementary school, their minds were receptive and moldable - - but what did they learn? Was there anything being taught to them that remotely related to what they were thinking and how they were feeling? Their antisocial actions as teenagers certainly reveal how troubled they must have been as small children. Were there no teachers to pick up on that? Or perhaps teachers did see these antisocial propensities in some of their students but were not trained to deal with them.

Teachers are required to follow a preplanned schedule of academic achievement for each grade level. A second grader, for example, needs to be on a certain level in reading, spelling and math before being promoted to the third grade. Teachers with too many students who fail to reach this promotional level are highly suspect of being incompetent, consequently, teachers must place a higher priority on teaching children the ABCs rather than on providing them with the favorable conditions they need for healthy emotional development.

Of course nothing can take the place of a loving home environment. Children who are fortunate enough to be genuinely loved most likely will grow up to be emotionally healthy adults, but it is not only love that promotes a child's healthy emotional development. Second to being loved, a child needs to be respected so that he can feel totally acceptable as he or she really is. The premise that children need love is true, but it can be very damaging as well because many caretakers, teachers, daycare providers, and even some parents pretend a love they do not really feel. They pretend it because they think it is servicing the child's needs, but to the contrary, it is actually damaging to the child's sense of self-worth and self-esteem.

A child cannot be easily fooled. If he is genuinely loved he will know it, but if the love is a pretense, he will know that too, and that is the damaging part. He sees the pretense but does not understand it. He will often interpret the pretense as an indication that he must not be acceptable as he really is, otherwise adults would not be relating to him with deception and insincerity.

Teachers, caretakers, relatives, etc., that is anyone who has a relationship with a child would best serve the child's interest by dealing with him honestly. If they do not love the child but pretend they do they should substitute their artificial love with genuine respect and start relating to the child in a way that will let him know there is nothing wrong with him - - he is "okay" as he is.

> The human individual needs favorable conditions for his growth... he needs an atmosphere of warmth to give him both a feeling of inner security and the inner freedom enabling him to have his own feelings and thoughts and to express himself. He needs the good will of others, not only to help him in his many needs but to guide him and encourage him to become a mature and fulfilled individual. (Karen Horney, 1950, p.18)

Ideally, parents and caretakers should be the "others who guide him and encourage him", but this is not the reality. Far too many parents do not provide their children with the kind of atmosphere that will promote their children's healthy emotional development. Some may want to, but they do not have the first clue about what they should do, primarily because they have never learned it themselves, neither at home nor in school.

In summary, the academics are important, but not in the minds of very young children. A well-adjusted child over the age of nine can learn all the material taught in the first, second, and third grades in a very short time period. Children attend elementary school at ages when their minds are open, receptive, and easily influenced. If the right persuasions do not come from the child's family or school, the wrong ones will come from other sources. Adolph Hitler was often quoted as saying, "Give me a child until he is nine and I will give you a Nazi for life." A well-trained teacher with a professionally planned curriculum can say, "Give me a child until he is nine and I will give you a well-adjusted adult for life."

An adult who is well-adjusted is better able to cope with life's trials and tribulations, some of which can be severe enough to undermine the security of even the most emotionally stable individuals. On the surface, many of us handle our hurtful circumstances with an attitude of "that's life", but beneath the surface, the pain we endure has a significant impact on our emotional health. Consequently, many of us have experienced moments and perhaps even periods of emotional unbalance or abnormal functioning. One renowned psychologist believed, "What is psychologically healthy in human beings is basically only qualitatively different from that which is unhealthy."[12] Another stated, the person who has achieved complete psychological health probably does not exist; these persons are rare indeed but the vast majority of people in the world have established a balance between normality and abnormality which leans more toward psychological health.[13]

How can a sensitive and alive person ever feel secure? Because of the very conditions of our existence, we cannot feel secure about anything. Our thoughts and insights are at best partial truths, mixed with a great deal of error, not to speak of the unnecessary misinformation about life and society to which we are exposed almost from the day of birth. Our life and our health are subject to accidents beyond our control. If we make a decision, we can never be sure of its outcome: any decision implies a risk of failure, and if it does not imply it, it has not been a decision in the true sense of the word. We can never be certain of the outcome of our best efforts. The result always depends on many factors which transcend our capacity of control. Just as a sensitive and alive person cannot avoid being sad, he cannot avoid feeling insecure. The psychic task which a person can and must set for himself is not to feel secure, but to be able to tolerate the insecurity, without panic and undue fear. (Erich Fromm, 1955, p.196)

Because no formal diagnosis exists for the various trials and tribulations we experience in our lives, these normal struggles and human difficulties are relegated to, and sometimes masked under, other existing mental and/or physical disorders. "The fact that we weep, that we carry sadness in our heart, is now a psychological 'problem' but clearly this is no psychological problem or issue; it is simple human sadness."[14]

We are so quick to use diagnosis as our first line of defense against listening to our true nature... Depression is a particularly popular diagnosis... We have learned to see ourselves as a random collection of symptoms. We put them in a pattern, correlate a diagnosis, and we feel we have named who we are. But this is not who we are; rather, it is simply one manifestation – and I would argue, a rather superficial and transitory one - of who we are beneath those symptoms. (Wayne Muller, 1996, p.31)

Identification and classification are fundamental to our need to order the world around us so that we can make sense of reality.[15] So we declare that some things belong in class A, and others in class non-A; but in some instances, it may be very difficult, or even impossible to establish in what class a particular item belongs.[16] Man is one of those particular items. Animals, vegetables, rocks, etc., may be very nicely organized and thus classified, but sometimes human behavior cannot be reduced to this or that or relegated to class A, or class non-A categories.[17] We are human, which means from birth to death we are in a constant state of change.

Although there is some utility in the proper study, diagnosis, and treatment of mental illness, the many individuals who are just psychologically hurting should not fall victim to this sterile and sometimes mechanistic and arbitrary classification system. Nevertheless, for some reason, some professionals feel compelled to diagnose and label every human problem they observe:

> *For some scientists, particularly those who work in the "personal" sciences of psychology, sociology, and anthropology, classical scientific method may serve the function of a defense mechanism. By abstracting, objectifying, and generally dehumanizing their human subjects, these scientific workers unconsciously seek to isolate themselves from the all-too-human failings, emotions, anxieties, and confusion they investigate in others. (Abraham Maslow, 1966, p.33)*

If all persons must be diagnosed with a label in order to get insurance coverage for their psychological treatment, then we should invent a new category for them e.g. "S.O.S. Trying to Emotionally Survive with Dysfunctional People in a Complex Society, and a Troubled World."

But how can we emotionally survive a complex society and a troubled world if we come from a dysfunctional and/ or unloving family. We may need someone to help. If we are without a trusted confidant who is able to help us, we must seek one out. Psychologists are not only trustworthy confidants, but they are also well-trained professionals who know how to help individuals deal with their problems and pain.

Some people just need someone to listen to them. Others need someone to help them recognize the underlying causes of their difficulties. For example, a wife can readily talk about her insomnia and depression but is emotionally unable to talk about the fact that she does not love her husband anymore. A man can spend hours talking about his back pain but is emotionally unable to talk about how it is making him unemployable and dependent. Parents are able to discuss the physical problems of their teenage daughter but are emotionally unable to discuss her eating disorder which is causing her physical problems. In short, psychologists help individuals identify and deal with the core issues that lie beneath the surface.

Historically, there was a negative social stigma attached to those who sought professional psychological help implying these individuals were somehow weak, deviant or abnormal. Society still tends to view these individuals as weak, yet nothing could be further from the truth. It is only the person who attempts to face himself who inherently possesses the greatest strength and courage. Carl Jung noted, "Whoever goes to himself risks a confrontation with himself and this confrontation is the first test of courage... a test sufficient to frighten most people." [18]

Self-knowledge facilitates the achievement of personal power which is the greatest power we can ever achieve. When we have this power, we need no other. We become the captain of our ship. We are able to sail on any course we desire. As Erich Fromm explained, personal strength is contingent upon developing a sense of identity based on the experience of one's own powers... to the extent which he grasps his own reality - - "*my* thoughts", "*my* decisions", "*my* judgments", "*my* actions" - - can he make his world his.[19]

> *Happiness consists in our touching the rock bottom of reality, in the discovery of our self ...To emerge from the ideas of infantile grandiosity into the conviction of one's real strength; to be able*

to accept the paradox that every one of us is the most important thing there is in the universe – and at the same time not more important than a fly or a blade of grass. To be able to tolerate uncertainty about the most important question with which life confronts us – and yet to have faith in our thought and feeling, insomuch as they are truly ours. (Erich Fromm, 1955, p.202-204)

Erich Fromm believed all forms of self-identity which are based on group membership or external sources make an individual dependent and weak.[20] Since a conformist never asks whether he is right or wrong but whether he is doing what everyone else is doing, he therefore thinks, "I must conform so I am not different or seen as peculiar".[21] Similarly, Nathaniel Branden noted, "Man makes himself worthy of living by making himself competent to live: by dedicating his mind to the task of discovering what is true and right, and by governing his actions accordingly."[22] In other words, he stands up for what he believes regardless of what others think or whatever the consequences may be. "Defeat in doing the right is nevertheless victory" - - or in the words of Martin Luther King, "My obligation is to do the right thing. The rest is in God's hands."

How can conscience develop when the principle of life is conformity? Conscience, by its very nature is nonconforming: it must be able to say no, when everybody else says yes…. To the degree to which a person conforms he cannot hear the voice of his conscience, much less act upon it. (Erich Fromm, 1955, p.173)

As we learn more about ourselves, we learn how to tolerate our many insecurities without panic and undue fear, and we learn how to direct our lives in spite of our many insecurities and fears or, perhaps, because of them. Pop psychology leads us to believe there are quick fixes and magic cures for whatever ails our souls but this form of "cookbook psychology" only serves to alienate us even further because it diverts our attention away not only from our true nature and our real emotions, but also from the real answers and insights we need to comfort and sustain us. We are bombarded with a never ending array of psychological recipes which promise to help us achieve happiness, self-confidence and self-esteem when in reality these attributes can only come from honest introspection and complete self-awareness.

In counseling or psychotherapy with a trained professional, a person learns about himself or herself as a unique individual. It is a personal journey into the unknown and undiscovered. In essence, it is a retrieval, resurrection, and restoration of the person's real self and, beyond this, it provides an opportunity for one to learn how to trust another person again. In counseling with a qualified professional, individuals learn they can psychologically expose themselves without being harmed, hurt or humiliated. This is how emotional healing begins.

It must be emphasized that the selection of a competent therapist is one of the most important decisions an individual will make in his or her entire life. Research consistently shows that bad therapy is worse than no therapy at all. As carefully as one would shop for a hairdresser, for a luxury, or for any valued item, one should do the same for a professional therapist, or for that matter, *any* professional. Psychologists are the most educated and well-trained therapists, since they possess a doctorate degree which requires up to twelve years or more of intensive study and training specifically in the field of psychology.

At the top of the list, one must be sure the professional is competent. Do not assume competence no matter what the degree or status. Equally important is the professional's ethical standards. Unfortunately, information about a professional's ethical standards can be difficult to obtain until it is too late but there are various cues which you can use to guide you.

First, you should always feel respected as a person and, if you do not, then you should terminate the relationship immediately. The professional should appear genuinely interested in your welfare and this interest can be demonstrated through various observable behaviors, e.g., maintains good eye contact, keeps appointments, follows through on his or her word, and is reasonably available to speak to, if necessary, outside of scheduled appointments. In simple terms, you should be able to "connect" with the professional who is providing a service to you. Trust your gut instincts.

> *Psychologists... are born, not made. Psychological interest and the gift of psychological observation are as inborn as a musical sense or a mathematical talent. Where it is not present, nothing - not even courses, lectures, and seminars - will produce it. The comparison with musicianship is justified in more than one sense. Musicians, like psychologists, are born; but, in order to become what they are, they must be trained and they must work long and hard. Talent alone is not enough; but work and industry alone, without talent are nothing. (Theodore Reik, 1948, p.13)*

In summary, we are all born with a monumental challenge. We must live the one life we are certain that we have, and we must overcome all the physical and emotional obstacles we encounter. We cannot hide, we cannot stick our heads in the sand, and we cannot emotionally shut down - - not if we want to feel alive, not if we want to feel love, and not if we want to feel some moments of happiness in our lives. We cannot compartmentalize that which we will feel and that which we will not. It is all or nothing and too many of us settle for nothing.

Erich Fromm believed our deepest emotional need is to overcome our separateness and to leave our prison of aloneness. Herein lies the ultimate psychological dilemma and the most perplexing challenge for every sensitive person who has been badly hurt by love and by life. Should he remain in his self-made prison and live the rest of his life alone, but with safety and protection from more emotional pain and sorrow, or should he make a plan to leave it - - a plan that may include many things, such as counseling, marital therapy, antidepressants, reliance on God or a Higher Power, friendship, fellowship, volunteer work, joining a group, or any combination thereof.

Anyone who has erected a brick wall around himself for emotional protection needs courage to remove the wall and become vulnerable again to more emotional pain. These brick walls rarely go up all at once. Usually they go up one brick at a time and this is the way to tear them down, that is, one brick at a time.

The first brick is removed simply by becoming more aware of your surrounding circumstances and being on constant watch for caring, kind, and compassionate people. At the same time, you must become more adept at recognizing hurtful people and toxic circumstances that caused you to put up your wall in the first place. If these hurtful people and circumstances cannot be avoided altogether, then at least by recognizing them, you will be better prepared to handle their emotional harpoons.

Ironically, it may have taken many hurtful people to force you into a prison of aloneness but it only takes one person to help you crawl out. If you can learn to trust just one other person, then you can generalize this trust onto others. When your trust is restored, even in small measure, your hope will be restored to the same extent. With even the slightest degree of trust and hope back in your heart, there is a renewed possibility that you could care about someone again - - that you could love someone again. It is precisely these renewed possibilities that help you leave your prison of aloneness.

In conclusion, you can slowly and ever so carefully tear down your wall, brick by brick, and open yourself up to all that will make your life more meaningful and fulfilling - - to friendship, fellowship, and the possibility of authentic love; or, you can continue to live the rest of your life alone in the safety and security of your self-made prison. It is a choice that every person must make for himself or herself - - a choice that must be deliberate and conscious because doing nothing is a choice in and of itself.

Doing nothing will leave you victimized by your past but more importantly, it will make you powerless over your future. As noted above, "For life to be meaningful and worthwhile, the individual must feel he has the power within himself to shape his own destiny." Everyone has this power within them but not everyone has the self-knowledge they need to feel it - - and to *use* it.

The best way to conclude this book is to summarize its core message. Look at the people in your life, both in the present as well as the past, and understand the influence they have had on your self-image. Look at the cultural values that you learned from our society and understand the effects they have had on your self-esteem. Look at the social ills and human cruelties that surround us in today's troubled world and understand the negative impact they have on your emotional security and sense of well-being.

Above all else, look at yourself and understand who you really are beneath the surface. Are you the unique individual you were born to be, or do you experience yourself entirely as the person you think you are supposed to be? Question whether or not your feelings are intact, that is, can you feel happiness as well as pain? Can you feel joy as well as sorrow? Can you love? Can you be loved? Do you have hope? If you can answer yes to all these questions - - then you are emotionally surviving.

A FINAL WORD TO THE READER:

Tragedy, betrayal and injustice can occur as a result of misplaced trust in an individual, agency, or service provider. The worst part about this truth is that unless an individual's damages are monetarily significant, and unless the victimization, incompetence, or maltreatment can be fully substantiated, there is little or no chance for justice or legal retribution.

Moreover, when women are victimized, it can be brutal if they try to seek justice or legal recourse. It is called, "The Nuts and Sluts Strategy": Defense attorneys argue that she's a nut, that is, she made the whole thing up or in cases of sexual harassment or sexual assault, she's a slut - - she asked for it, she enjoyed it.[1] The idea is to inflict so much emotional pain on the victims that it will persuade them to withdraw their case or settle for very little.[2]

If anyone has had such an experience, I would be interested in hearing your story. I would also be interested in hearing about any unsuccessful services that were specifically directed toward psychological and/or physical improvement such as therapeutic, cosmetic, and dietary interventions. Your story will be kept in strictest confidence and it can be told under an alias name if preferred. The service provider's name and address are desired. In addition, a way to contact you personally is preferred, but of course optional. Be assured that nothing will be done with your shared story without your verbal permission and signed consent.

Finally, your confidential disclosure may help someone else or possibly spare someone else from your unfortunate experience. Please consider this fact in your important decision to disclose your personal story.

You can confidentially share your experience with me by e-mailing me at: survivalbook@comcast.net

REFERENCES

CHAPTER 1. THE IDEAL SELF:

Quote 1: Fromm, E. (1955). The sane society. Henry Holt and Company: New York, New York. p. 16

1. Fromm, E. (1955). The sane society. Henry Holt and Company: New York, New York. p. 144

2. 3. & 4. Monte, C. (1977). Beneath the mask. Holt, Rhinehart, and Winston: New York. p.495 (citing Erich Fromm)

Quote 2: Jung, C. (1938). Psychology and religion. Yale University Press, Inc.: New Haven and London. p.60

5., 6., 7., 8., & 9. Horney, K. (1950). Neurosis and human growth. W.W. Norton & Company, Inc.: New York. p.138

10. Fromm, E. (1955). The sane society. Henry Holt and Company: New York, New York. p. 139

11.& 12. Monte, C. (1977). Beneath the mask. Holt, Rhinehart, and Winston: New York. p.565 (citing Abraham Maslow)

13. Horney, K. (1950). Neurosis and human growth. W.W. Norton & Company, Inc.: New York. p.137

14. Horney, K. (1950). <u>Neurosis and human growth</u>. W.W. Norton & Company, Inc.: New York. p.110

15. Horney, K. (1950). <u>Neurosis and human growth</u>. W.W. Norton & Company, Inc.: New York. p.112

POEM: "Entwicklungsschmerzen" by Christian Moganstern Collection of Poems Auf vielen Wegen, R. Piper and Co., Munich 1921 Translation of this poem by Caroline Newton. Poem also cited inHorney, K. (1950). <u>Neurosis and human growth</u>. W.W. Norton & Company, Inc.: New York. p.113-114

16. Horney, K. (1950). <u>Neurosis and human growth</u>. W.W.Norton & Company, Inc.: New York. p.112

17. Horney, K. (1950). <u>Neurosis and human growth</u>. W.W.Norton & Company, Inc.: New York. p.110

18. Horney, K. (1950). <u>Neurosis and human growth</u>. W.W.Norton & Company, Inc.: New York. p.111

Quote 2: Horney, K. (1950). <u>Neurosis and human growth</u>. W.W. Norton & Company, Inc.: New York. p.110

19. Monte, C. (1977). <u>Beneath the mask</u>. Holt,Rinehart, and Winston: New York. p.62 (citing Sigmund Freud)

20. Horney, K. (1950). <u>Neurosis and human growth</u>. W.W.Norton & Company, Inc.: New York. p.117

21. & 22. Horney, K. (1950). <u>Neurosis and human growth</u>. W.W. Norton & Company, Inc.: New York. p.356-357

23. 24., 25. & 26. Adler, A. (1973). Superiority and Social Interest: A Collection of Latter Writings. H.L. Ansbacher and R.R. Ansbacher (Eds.). Viking Books: New York.

27. Fromm, E. (1955). The sane society. Henry Holt and Company: NewYork, New York, p.143

28. Fromm, E.

29. & 30. Fromm, E. (1955). The sane society. Henry Holt and Company: NewYork, p.144

Quote 3: Horney, K. (1950). Neurosis and human growth. W.W.Norton & Company, Inc.: New York. p.26

CHAPTER 2. KNOW THYSELF:

Quote 1: Fromm, E. (1941). Escape from Freedom. Avon Books: New York. p.275

1. James, M. & Ward, J. (1971). Born to win. Addison-Wesley Publishing Company, Inc.: New York. p.36

2. James, M. & Ward, J. (1971). Born to win. Addison-Wesley Publishing Company, Inc. New York. p.49

3 & 4. James, M & Ward, J. (1971). Born to win. Addison-Wesley Publishing Company, Inc.: New York. p.53

5. & 6. Horney, K. (1950). Neurosis and human growth. W.W. Norton & Company, Inc.: New York. pp.202-203

7. & 8. Monte, C. (1977). <u>Beneath the mask</u>. Holt, Rinehart, and Winston: New York. pp.585-586 (citing Carl Rogers)

Quote 2: Horney, K. (1950). <u>Neurosis and human growth</u>. W.W. Norton & Company, Inc.: New York pp.18, 20-23

9. Goleman, D. (1995). <u>Emotional intelligence</u>. Bantam Books: New York Toronto London Sydney Auckland. p.60

10. Branden, N. (1969). <u>The psychology of self-esteem</u>. Bantam Books: New York. p.viii

11. Branden, N. (1969). <u>The psychology of self-esteem.</u> Bantam Books: New York. p.110

Quote 3: Branden, N. (1969). <u>The psychology of self-esteem.</u> Bantam Books: New York. p.110

Quote 4: Soren Kierkegaard, 1941

12.& 13. Monte, C. (1977). <u>Beneath the mask</u>. Holt, Rinehart, and Winston: NewYork. p.23

Quote 5: Monte, C. (1977). <u>Beneath the mask</u>. Holt, Rinehart, and Winston: New York. p.566 (citing Abraham Maslow)

Maslow, Abraham. (1966). <u>The psychology of science</u>: <u>A reconnaissance</u>. New York: Harper & Row. P.16

14. Monte, C. (1977). <u>Beneath the mask</u>. Holt, Rinehart, and Winston: New York. p.61 (citing Sigmund Freud)

15. 16. & 17. Monte, C. (1977). <u>Beneath the mask</u>. Holt, Rinehart, and Winston: New York. p.353 (Jean Piaget)

Quote 6: Horney, K. (1950). <u>Neurosis and human growth.</u> W.W. Norton & Company, Inc.: New York pp.17-18

CHAPTER 3. EMOTIONAL PAIN AND SORROW:

Quote 1. Monte, C. (1977). <u>Beneath the mask</u>. Holt, Rhinehart, and Winston: New York: p.486. (citing Erich Fromm)

Quote 2: Fromm, E. (1955). <u>The sane society.</u> Holt, Rinehart and Winston: New York. p.201

1. Frankl, V. (1959). <u>Mans search for meaning.</u> Washington Square Press. Pocket Books, a division of Simon & Schuster Inc.: New York p.124-125

2. Frankl, V. (1959). <u>Mans search for meaning</u>. Washington Square Press. Pocket Books, a division of Simon & Schuster Inc.: New York p.125

Quote 3: Branden, N. (1969). <u>The psychology of self-esteem.</u> Bantam Books: New York. p.90

3. Beck, A. (1988). <u>Love is never enough.</u> Harper & Row Publishers: New York. p.146

4. Catherall, D. (1992). <u>Back from the brink: A family guide to overcoming traumatic stress.</u> Bantam Books: New York Toronto London Sydney Auckland. p.96

5. Muller, W. (1996). How then shall we live? Bantam Books: New York Toronto London Sydney Auckland. p.25

Quote 4: Frankl, V. (1959). Mans search for meaning. Washington Square Press. Pocket Books, a division of Simon & Schuster Inc.: New York p.88

6. 7. & 8. Goleman, D. (1995). Emotional intelligence. Bantam Books: New York Toronto London Sydney Auckland. p.138-139

9.& 10. Catherall, D. (1992). Back from the brink:A family guide to overcoming traumaticstress. Bantam Books: New York Toronto London Sydney Auckland. P.38

Quote 5: Catherall, D. (1992). Back from the brink: A family guide to overcoming traumatic stress. Bantam Books: New York Toronto London Sydney Auckland. pp.2-43

11. Goleman, D. (1995). Emotional intelligence. Bantam Books: New York Toronto London Sydney Auckland. p.202

12. Rogers, C. (1965). Client-centered therapy. Houghton-Mifflin: Boston. p.104

13. Goleman, D. (1995). Emotional intelligence. Bantam Books: New York Toronto London Sydney Auckland. p.209

14. Monte, C. (1977). Beneath the mask. Holt, Rhinehart, and Winston: New York. p.92

15., 16.,17., & 18. Kushner, H. (1981). <u>When bad things happen to good people</u>. Avon Books: New York. p.92

Quote 5: Kushner, H. (1981). <u>When bad things happen to good people</u>. Avon Books: New York. p.87

19. Frankyl, V. (1959). <u>Mans search for meaning</u>.
Washington Square Press Publication of Pocket Books,
a division of Simon & Shuster Inc.: New York. p.126

Quote 6: Muller, W. (1996). <u>How then shall we live?</u> Bantam Books: New York Toronto London Sydney Auckland. p.26

CHAPTER 4. REGAINING TRUST AND HOPE:

1. Monte, C. (1977). <u>Beneath the mask</u>. Holt, Rhinehart, and Winston: New York. p.246. (citing Erik Erikson)

2. Erikson, E. (1950). <u>Childhood and society</u>.
W.W. Norton & Company: New York. p. 249

3. Monte, C. (1977). <u>Beneath the mask</u>. Holt, Rhinehart, and Winston: New York. p.7 (citing Harry Stack Sullivan)

4. 5. & 6. Monte, C. (1977). <u>Beneath the mask</u>. Holt, Rhinehart, and Winston: New York. p.247 (citing Erik Erikson)

Erikson, E. (1964). <u>Insight and responsibility.</u>
W.W. Norton & Company: New York. p.118

7. Fromm, E.

8. & 9. Beck, A., Rush, A., Shaw, B. & Emery, G. (1979). Cognitive therapy of depression. The Guilford Press: New York. p.11

10. Myers, D. (1992). The pursuit of happiness. New York: Avon Books p.189

11&12. Myers, D. (1992). The pursuit of happiness. New York: Avon Books pp.147, 186-187 (citing Martin Seligman)

Seligman, M. (1988). "Why is there so much depression today"? In G. Stanley Hall Lectures, edited by I. S. Cohen. Vol. 9, Washington, DC. American Psychological Association. Seligman, M. (1988). "Boomer Blues". Psychology Today, Oct. 50-55

13. Websters College Dictionary 1989, p.589

14. Branden, N. (1969). The psychology of self-esteem. Bantam Books: New York. p.90

15. Monte, C. (1977). Beneath the mask. Holt, Rhinehart, and Winston: New York. p.491 (citing Erich Fromm)

16. Monte, C. (1977). Beneath the mask. Holt, Rhinehart, and Winston. New York. p.493 (citing Erich Fromm)

17. & 18. Monte, C. (1977). Beneath the mask. Holt, Rhinehart, and Winston: New York. p.22 (citing George Kelly)

19. Monte, C. (1977). Beneath the mask. Holt, Rhinehart, and Winston: New York. pp.436-437 (George Kelly)

Kelly, G. (1955). The Psychology of personal Constructs, Vols. 1 & 2 Norton: New York

20. Fromm, E. (1956). The art of loving. Bantam Books: New York. p.8

21. Fromm, E. (1955). The sane society. Holt, Rinehart and Winston: New York. p.33

Poem: Julian Green, Personal Record, 1928-1939, translated by J. Godefroi, Harper & Brothers, New York, 1939. Taken from: Fromm, E. (1941). Escape from freedom. Avon Books: New York. p. 154

CHAPTER 5. THE PARADOX OF LOVE:

Quote 1: Mother Teresa (1995). A simple faith. Ballantine Books: New York. p.79

1. Maslow, A. (1971). The farther reaches of human nature. Viking Books: New York.p.17

2. Fromm, E. (1956). The art of loving. Bantam Books: New York. p.4

3. Fromm, E. (1956). The art of loving. Bantam Books: New York. p.3

4.& 5. Fromm, E. (1956). The art of loving. Bantam Books: New York. pp.2-3

6.& 7. Horney, K. (1967). <u>Feminine psychology</u>. W W. Norton and Company, Inc.: New York. p.108

8. Frankl, V. (1959). <u>Mans search for meaning</u>. Washington Square Press. Pocket Books, a division of Simon & Schuster Inc.: New York. p.130

Quote 2: Fromm, E. (1956). <u>The art of loving</u>. Bantam Books: New York. pp. 45- 46, 10

9. Horney, K. (1967). <u>Feminine psychology</u>. W W. Norton and Company, Inc.: New York p.109

10. Fromm, E. (1956). <u>The art of loving</u>. Bantam Books: New York. p.4

11. Horney, K. (1967). <u>Feminine psychology</u>. W W. Norton and Company, Inc.: New York p.110

12. & 13. Horney, K.

Quote 3: Fromm, E. (1956). <u>The art of loving</u>. Bantam Books: New York. pp.2, 4, & 5

CHAPTER 6. RECLAIMING YOUR SOUL:

Quote 1: Frankl, V. (1959). <u>Mans search for meaning</u>. Washington Square Press. Pocket Books, a division of Simon & Schuster Inc.: New York pp.127

1. Myers, D. (1992). The pursuit of happiness. Avon Books: New York. p.189 (citing Martin Seligman)

Quote 2: Frankl, V. (1959). Mans search for meaning. Washington Square Press. Pocket Books, a division of Simon & Schuster Inc.: New York p.126

2. Branden, N. (1969). The psychology of self- esteem. Bantam Books: New York. p.66

Quote 3: Branden, N. (1969). The psychology of self- esteem. Bantam Books: New York. pp.66-67

Quote 4: Branden, N. (1969). The psychology of self- esteem. Bantam Books: New York. p.67

3. Author unknown.

4. 5. & 6. Myers, D. (1992). The pursuit of happiness. Avon Books. New York. p.192

Quote 5: Kushner, H. (1981). When bad things happen to good people. Avon Books: New York. p.10

7. Frankl, V. (1959). Mans search for meaning. Washington Square Press. Pocket Books, a division of Simon & Schuster Inc.: New York pp.128-129

8. Myers, D. (1992). The pursuit of happiness. Avon Books New York. p.189 (citing Rabbi Kushner)

9. Monte, C. (1977). Beneath the mask. Holt, Rinehart,

and Winston: New York. p.493 (citing Erich Fromm)

10. Monte, C. (1977). <u>Beneath the mask</u>. Holt, Rinehart, and Winston: New York p.301 (citing Carl Jung)

11. Myers, D. (1992). <u>The pursuit of happiness</u>. Avon Books: New York. p.204

Quote 6: Frankl, V. (1959). <u>Mans search for meaning</u>. Washington Square Press. Pocket Books, a division of Simon & Schuster Inc.: New York pp.86-87

Quote 7: Muller, W. (1996). <u>How then shall we live</u>? Bantam Books: New York Toronto London Sydney Auckland. p.235 (citing Mother Teresa)

12. & 13. Mother Teresa (1995). <u>A simple faith</u>. Ballantine Books: New York.p.65

14. Smedes, L. (1996). The art of forgiving. Ballantine Publishing Group: New York. pp. 175

Quote 8: Smedes, L. (1996). <u>The art of forgiving</u>. Ballantine Publishing Group: New York. pp. 171,174

15. & 16 Muller, W. (1996). <u>How then shall we live</u>? Bantam Books: New York Toronto London Sydney Auckland. p.205

17. Fromm, E. (1955). <u>The sane society</u>. Holt, Rinehart and Winston: New York. p.122

18. Myers, D. (1992). The pursuit of happiness. Avon Books: New York. p.192

CHAPTER 7. PSYCHOLOGY AND ITS PURPOSE:

Quote 1: Fromm, E. (1955). The sane society. Holt, Rinehart and Winston: New York. pp. 170-171

1. Monte, C. (1977). Beneath the mask. Holt, Rinehart, and Winston: New York. p.550 (citing Abraham Maslow)

2. Monte, C. (1977). Beneath the mask. Holt, Rinehart, and Winston: New York. p.573 (citing Carl Rogers)

3. Monte, C. (1977). Beneath the mask. Holt, Rinehart, and Winston: New York. p.300 (citing Carl Jung)

4. Monte, C. (1977). Beneath the mask. Holt, Rinehart, and Winston: New York. p.318 (citing Alfred Adler)

5. Monte, C. (1977). Beneath the mask. Holt, Rinehart, and Winston: New York. p.236 (citing Erik Erikson)

Quote 4: Fromm, E. (1955). The sane society. Holt, Rinehart and Winston: New York. p.141-142

Quote 5: Fromm, E. (1956). The art of loving. Bantam Books: New York. p.14

6. Monte, C. (1977). Beneath the mask. Holt, Rinehart, and Winston: New York. p.486 (citing Erich Fromm)

7. Monte, C. (1977). Beneath the mask. Holt, Rinehart, and Winston: NewYork. p.484 (citing Erich Fromm)

8. & 9. Fromm, E. (1955). The sane society. Holt, Rinehart and Winston: New York. p.12

10. Fromm, E. (1955). The sane society. Holt, Rinehart and Winston: New York. p.72

11. Fromm, E. (1955). The sane society. Holt, Rinehart and Winston: New York. p.19

Quote 6: Fromm, E. (1955). The sane society. Holt, Rinehart and Winston: New York. p.72-73, 19

Quote 7: Quote 2: Branden, N. (1969). The psychology of self-esteem. Bantam Books: New York. p. 90

Quote 8: Horney, K. (1950). Neurosis and human growth. W.W. Norton & Company: New York. p.18

12. Horney, K. (1950). Neurosis and human growth. W.W. Norton & Company: New York. p.4

13. Monte, C. (1977). Beneath the mask. Holt, Rinehart, and Winston: New York. p.550 (citing Abraham Maslow)

Quote 9: Fromm, E. (1955). The sane society. Holt, Rinehart and Winston: New York. p.196

14. Muller, W. (1996). How then shall we live? Bantam Books: New York Toronto London Sydney Auckland. p.19

Quote 10: Muller, W. (1996). How then shall we live? Bantam Books: New York. p.31

15. & 16. Szasz, T. (1974). The myth of mental illness. Harper and Row Publishers: New York. p.33

17. Szasz, T. (1974). The myth of mental illness. Harper and Row Publishers: New York. p.34

Quote 11: Monte, C. (1977). Beneath the mask. Holt, Rinehart, and Winston: New York. p.566 (citing Abraham Maslow)

Maslow, A. (1966) The Psychology of Science: A Reconnaissance. Harper Row: New York. p.33

18. Jung, C. (1936) Archetypes of the Collective Unconscious, Vol. 9 of the Collected Works of C.G. Jung. Princeton University Press; Princeton, N.J.

19. Fromm, E. (1955). The sane society. Holt, Rinehart and Winston: New York. pp.69,143

Quote 12: Fromm, E. (1955). The sane society. Holt, Rinehart and Winston: New York. p.202-204

20. Fromm, E. (1955). The sane society. Holt, Rinehart and Winston: New York. p.69

21. Fromm, E. (1955). The sane society. Holt, Rinehart and Winston: New York. p.153

22. Branden, N. (1969). <u>The psychology of self-esteem.</u> Bantam Books: New York: p.114

Quote 13: Reik, T. (1948). <u>Listening with the third ear.</u> Jove Publications Inc. : New York. p.13

FINAL WORD TO THE READER:

1. & 2. Steiber, T. (1996). The Nuts and Sluts Strategy. New Woman Magazine. August

EMOTIONAL SURVIVAL